The Principles Of Life

All you need to know to live the best life ever!

by

Steve Norton

Printed by
Antony Rowe Limited

First published in the UK by
Steven Norton

First published 2002.

ISBN 0-9541954-0-X

Printing services provided by

Antony Rowe Limited
Bumpers Farm industrial estate
Chippenham
Wiltshire
SN14 6LH

FOR GRANDAD

I had one person who truly believed in me, it was you Grandad.
That was all it took.
Love always
Stevo

Contents

Contents

FOREWORD

It was 1999 when I finished it; at that time I didn't realise that I had anything better than some good advice on two pieces of paper. Little did I know that those two pieces of paper and the explanation that went with them would herald a whole new way to treat my clients which could cut the standard therapy time to about a third of its usual time, with outrageously good results.

My idea was to sit down and devise a system or plan for my clients to follow so that I could give them something to take away and think about. So this is what I did. It took about a month to do but at the end I was quite happy with the result. These principles were born out of all the knowledge from many sources that I had learned and gained experience from since the early 1990s. I would give my clients the **"At a Glance Principles of Life"** on two sheets of paper to take away after their first session with me, without even explaining what they were. At the following session, a week later, I would give a 90-minute explanation of the principles, giving examples of how clients could incorporate them into their lives. What I found, though, was that some of those people who came to see me after the first session were coming back the following week already changed — without the explanation! Some of these people were turning up at first as emotional wrecks, without a real purpose in their lives, but were coming back the following week totally transformed. But what really was the icing on the cake was when I actually went through the principles with them and explained them. For some of those people it was like the parting of the clouds where the sun was now able to shine as, for probably the first time in their lives, they had a map of how to live their lives.

I realised that these people had been to school and some of them had achieved excellent qualifications but nobody had schooled them on how to run their bodies and minds to achieve the same excellent results. This stuff was blowing them away and it was exactly what they needed to hear. At last the map was in their hands: **The Principles Of Life**. Of course, not every client liked to hear what was said when I explained the principles and some of the most reactive of them refused to be schooled by them. That's always the case, though: you cannot help those who don't really want to change. The one's who did want to change, even though sometimes coming to see me in tatters beforehand, would become remarkably better within a few weeks after applying the principles. Whenever a relapse occurred it was **ALWAYS** due to people becoming lazy with the principles and forgetting to use them. I had a choice at this point: I could try to explain to every person who needed help in the world what the principles are (which would probably take up the rest of my life) or I could write this book and give you the full, uninterrupted three-hour version here. Obviously, I opted for the latter.

Unlike a lot of books which cover the topic of psychology, this book you will find easy to read and without any confusing jargon. It was written with **you** in mind, as I wanted to give you the easiest and most powerful source, which would be as good as seeing me personally. It is also a very cost-effective way of helping yourself, especially if you are living in Australia, as a trip to the UK to see me personally would cost a lot of money! Unlike many books on psychology and personal development, this book is not 400 pages long. This is because I have cut through the garbage and broken the information down so that it can be absorbed and applied as soon as you read it. Every word and every sentence is important and should be absorbed as nothing is left out and also nothing is drawn out to make this book larger than it needs to be. Instead, the information contained here will begin to change the way that you think, the way that you feel and the way you view your life — for the better.

Even if your life is OK and you feel happy, there is still much to learn in this book. If your life isn't OK, though, and you feel that it must change, then help is at hand. All you need to do is read this book, absorb the information and follow the exercises contained in each chapter.

Have fun!

Introduction

Welcome to the Principles of Life. Since 1995 I have been working as a therapist, helping many people with many problems such as low self-esteem, confidence problems, anxiety and stress, phobias, behavioural problems and just about any other problems people face.

In that time I've had the opportunity to learn from every one of over a thousand clients I have worked with and helped. I have also studied and read over a hundred books on psychology and personal development and listened to hundreds of audio tapes on the same subject from some of the world's most respected and renowned authors and speakers. People like Anthony Robbins, Richard Carlson, Dr Wayne Dyer, Ed Foreman and many others have helped me shape my life with the simple philosophies they shared with me through their books and audio tapes. Although I have lost count of the number of "personal development" tapes I have thrown in the bin!

Who needs personal development?

We live in a time where people are constantly seeking help for solving problems and difficulties, whether they be personal or professional. In the past, people would spend years trying to acquire knowledge through sometimes bitter experience of what to do or how to do things. This traditional way, although noble, is dated and should not be the way we acquire information today. People have gone before us and made the mistakes and gathered all of those years of knowledge and experience so that we don't have to do the same. We can, if we want to, use the information that they have learned and use it for ourselves without having to go through the same experiences that they had. That's called taking the short cut! We now live in an information age where information is (at the moment) the world's biggest industry. Information that used to be available to only a select few is now available on your home computer or at your local bookshop. Personal development is one such way in which we can learn to improve ourselves without having to go through the pitfalls of trial and error. This is such a valuable and essential commodity to use now that all leading companies and businesses use it for themselves and their staff. So much so, in fact, that any person or company who doesn't believe in personal development is literally the dinosaur still walking the Earth (and we all know what happened to the dinosaurs!). Unfortunately, I have found that the people who scoff at the idea of personal development are usually the ones who need it the most. Personal development is not a buzzword that will go away in time: it is the way forward for the future. Those who refuse to use it or say narrow-minded things about it are the ones who will struggle in years to come. It's like when people moan about the fast pace of technology that we have and say that they won't be part of it. To them I say this: you cannot win with this one as technology is not going to go away or slow down to suit you, so the sooner you realise that and get up to date, the easier your life will be in the future. Recently I heard a guy bragging smugly that he would never learn to use e-mail; this type of personality will be in deep trouble in the future and he will have only himself to blame for that. Personally, I think that technology is moving too slowly; this is because I am ahead of the game.

You see, personal development can be such a minefield. Who do you listen to? Which philosophy is best? Which will tell me what I really need to know about developing myself without filling me with confusing jargon? Well, the answer is here! What I have here for you is the only personal development blueprint you will ever need, taken from my own extensive experience, working with over a thousand clients, reading and listening to all those personal development audio-tapes and attending all those seminars. The following information has taken me years to acquire and cost me thousands of pounds so that I can bring it to you. That's right — I've done it all for you! You don't have to qualify as a therapist, see all the clients I have seen, read all those books or listen to all those tapes because I have distilled all that information for you, and created the ultimate success formula, which I call:

The Principles of Life

Before we go on with the principles, it is very important that we make some things very clear; the information covered next is some stuff I learned myself through my own findings, and some stuff I learned from other people in the personal development business. All I can say is this:

THE INFORMATION CONTAINED IN THE FOLLOWING TEXT HAS BEEN TRIED AND TESTED BY ME AND MY CLIENTS AND IS 100 PER CENT CAST IRON.

These principles which I am going to instil in you, are also used by every successful, happy person the world over, without question.

Another thing that people say to me quite often when they come to see me is that they have read personal development books before and that "They didn't work". Let me set the record straight once and for all with this issue. The information contained in the writings of, say, *Awaken the Giant Within* or *Stop Thinking and Start Living* is 100 per cent accurate and **if applied** you will get the results that they claim. But what some people think, is that if you read the book or listen to the tape then somehow your life will magically change without you having to do anything about it! Yes, it will make sense but **not doing anything** with that information will **not yield any results**. The books can only show you the way: they're just pieces of paper if you don't **take action** on the advice given. The same applies to this book. You must absorb this information, memorise it and use it every day so that it becomes a habit. Then your life **WILL CHANGE** — I guarantee it. Some of these principles you will be using already, some of them you will not. The ones you do not use now, I want you to adopt as soon as you read them — within 48 hours of reading them — because if you don't do it right away you will probably forget them. It is essential that after you read something in this book that tells you to do something, you do it **right away.** Whether it's a mental exercise or a writing exercise, you must put the book down and do it.

Some of the strategies and philosophies will challenge your current thinking, which is a good thing as, if you didn't need that to happen, then you wouldn't have bought this book in the first place. There are not many things in life that are truly guaranteed but this is my guarantee to you: adopting these principles will make your life ten times better. I'm not saying that your life isn't good now; I'm just saying that **IT WILL be ten times better** if you live your life by these principles. These principles are not a "pick and choose" list, though. If you really want to have the best life ever, you must adopt **ALL** of the principles and not just the ones that are the type you think you could do. The result of absorbing these principles and living your life by them is that a new state of mind and body is born. A new inner peace and self-confidence will emerge, which will colour the way you live your life forever. I call this new mental and physical state "**NO DOUBT**". It is an unstoppable self-confidence, which is within you but is rarely shared by the everyday people that you meet. Do not fear this new state of mind, as I believe it is your birthright to have it.

The **NO DOUBT** mindset is the end-product of absorbing and applying **ALL** of the principles of this book. These principles are not designed to be read once and then forgotten, with the hope that they will keep on working for you even though you no longer live your life by them. You do not take your car for a service and then say that it will now run well for the rest of its working life without any further maintenance, do you? Of course not: you know that to keep your car running in good order you have to maintain it regularly. You must do the same with these principles.

You cannot get lazy with these principles because if you begin to miss even one out it will start to have an effect somewhere in your life. It is like taking a leg off a table. With one away it starts to wobble; take two away and it will collapse.

Don't get lazy with these principles: you must live by them all!

NO DOUBT.

You'll get out of this book what you put in; nothing more, nothing less

Having said that, though, do not be surprised if your mindset begins to change all by itself. Whenever we read something as powerful as what you are about to read, it cannot fail to rub off on you in some way. If you're absolutely serious that you want to make some very positive changes in your mindset, everything you could ever need in order to do that is in this book. There is the "why you do it" and the "how to change it" for every challenge that you may have that is preventing you from really succeeding in your life. Sometimes you need to follow a certain mental exercise outlined in this book; other times you have to buy into a simple truth or philosophy in order to do it. Whatever it is or whatever the challenge may be, there is a solution somewhere in this book. No stone is left unturned. The goal of this book is to take you away from being a conscious mind thinker to become subconscious wisdom-driven instead. Do not worry what this means as it will become clearer and make more sense to you as you read this book.

Well if you're ready to change your life and you can't wait a second longer, let's begin! Let me show you how!

"I do not expect you to believe everything that I am about to present to you; the only thing I do ask is that you open your mind to the possibility of it."

Steve Norton

NO DOUBT

Whenever a person truly conquers his or her mind, a new state of mental being is born. I call this state NO DOUBT.
At this point the person with this mindset is an extremely powerful human being. This person has reversed the common way of using the conscious mind for 95 per cent of their thinking and only 5 per cent subconscious inner wisdom thinking, to that of subconscious inner wisdom 75 per cent and conscious mind 25 per cent. The conscious mind is no longer used for making important decisions and this faculty is now redundant for these means.

When a person has progressed into the realms of NO DOUBT, as the name might suggest, this person no longer suffers from insecurity and self-doubt. This person has no fear of doing whatever is needed to accomplish what they see as their goals and thinks of them as foregone conclusions, as the idea of not achieving their goals is not an option. Obstacles are of no bearing to whether a task is done or not. The mindset is <u>not</u> of "I don't think I can do it" or "I hope I can do it", but that of "I KNOW I can do it, and I have NO DOUBT it will occur". This mindset may seem preposterous to somebody who doesn't have it but every dynamic person lives by it. This state of being usually takes some time to build up within the individual and must be cultivated by constantly studying the personal development champions of past and present and learning from them. Often the road to NO DOUBT is constantly tested, with the conscious mind always trying to sabotage the journey, but full commitment to the cause and an unshakeable resolve are always the overriding factors. The person with the NO DOUBT mental state is <u>ultra-confident</u> but this should not be mistaken for the loud, cocky personality. The NO DOUBT personality doesn't suffer the low self-esteem need to prove to him- or herself or to others that they are indeed confident by appearing to be over-confident or loud. It is the KNOWING and not wanting that is the characteristic of a NO DOUBT personality. It's never a question of if but of WHEN.

NO DOUBT

Chapter One

Principle 1: You Own You!

Somebody once asked me why I got into personal development and I replied with "I had to — I had to do something to sort my life out". I was a strange kid: very nervous, and I had very low self-esteem. I hated myself and I thought life had dealt me a poor hand: I was in the self-pity mindset. I suffered terribly with my nerves when I was younger and I felt totally helpless and powerless within the life I was living. I had a real problem speaking correctly and my nerves were so bad I could hardly sit still. I **thought** that the life I was living was just the way things were going to be for me forever. At that point I didn't even know that with the right knowledge and guidance we could help change ourselves completely, so that the person we are could grow to be so much more. I would imagine my future life with these old behaviours **still** with me, and that would really scare me. I had never heard of personal development back then.

I want you to know that back in those dark days when I hated myself and my life I could never imagine that life could be as good as the one I am living today. Back then, I began to make some big decisions about changing my behaviours. The first step to turning my life around was making those decisions. Every day it felt like I was climbing a mountain but with sheer perseverance I managed to change myself into the person I now love. I do not write this because I want your sympathy or because this is still an "issue" with me, because it is not. I write this to show how, even if you think you are as low as you can go, with effort you can turn the whole thing around. As bad as it may be, it **can** change. You **can** become the person you want to be — you just need to know what to do in order for it to happen.

The other day I was speaking to a guy who told me that we are what we are and we can't change that fact. He said that if you're an unconfident person then that's the way it is. He said that if a person has learning difficulties, then that's just genetic. In the past I would have argued the point with him, with many counter-arguments to try to change his opinion, but instead I just smiled and said "O.K.". The fact that I didn't argue is testimony to the fact that we **can** change ourselves because otherwise I would have argued, as I would have done when I was younger and less wise. When a belief system is as strong as this it makes people blinkered to any other possibility. If this man were correct, I had better recall my successful clients!

Nothing is impossible to change. This is what you have to do to start to make it happen.

You need to know and fully understand that **you** are totally responsible for your life. Whether you're having a great life or not, it is **your responsibility**. If things aren't working for you in whatever area, it is up to **you** to sort it out. That doesn't mean that you can't get some help with it; it just means that you have to take the responsibility for changing it. The name used for describing what I mean is "being proactive". This is a term used often in business but seldom used by us everyday folk. What it means is that to be proactive **you** understand that **you** are responsible for your own happiness, your life, your health, and the direction in which your life is heading. If you're not happy with the way things are going, then it is up to **you** to take full responsibility for changing it. This can seem a little daunting at first but once you get the hang of it, let me tell you that it brings with it a tremendous feeling of freedom and self-confidence. Lack of self-confidence represents a large chunk of the problems for which my personal clients seek help.

Do not worry about taking full responsibility for yourself, as it will yield great things when you do.

To be proactive means that you **never blame** your parents, your upbringing, the area you live in, the economy, your partner, your schooling or any other circumstances for your not feeling happy in your life. Instead you accept them, as just **events** that in the past have been present in your life. How we **react** to a circumstance or event in our life now is **our** responsibility. That doesn't mean that if, for instance, you were abused as a child you were responsible for that or to blame for that — not at all, but what it does mean is that you are responsible **now** for how you live your life **after that**. How much it affects you **now** is your responsibility. That may seem a little tough, but it's the way it has to be. A proactive person ***is*** a tough cookie!

It's time to grow up

When we take full and utter responsibility for ourselves then we have truly grown up. This is not to be mistaken with becoming stuffy or too serious; in fact, quite the opposite. All it means is that we now are moving away from our old, immature behaviours and into a new personal freedom. Nor does this mean that we have to become over-sensible or old-minded. What I am saying is that if you are still using some old negative character traits or behaviours that are immature and inappropriate, now, as an adult, then it's time to do something about it. Some of those immature character traits that need to grow up are:

Jealousy; unnecessary fear and worry; childish behaviour; aggressive behaviour; tantrums; hysteria; moodiness; sulking; telling tales; whining that life isn't fair; bitching about others; hypochondria; sexual deviances; getting over annoyed; and any other immature behaviours

It's time to leave these immature behaviours behind where they belong — in the schoolyard! Making the decision to grow up and take full responsibility for the whole of your life can instantly eliminate these and other childish behaviours. The sooner you move away from them, the sooner you can start living with unbelievable self-confidence. These behaviours, although habitual, can easily be reversed by making a true commitment to do so. Many clients come to see me exhibiting such childish behaviours and are quite shocked when I tell them it's time to grow up. It's time to stop playing the "blame game" where everything that goes wrong is the fault of something or someone else. Some people believe or have been told that their behaviours are not actually caused by themselves but are in fact due to an "inner child" which is dictating them. This theory is a godsend to the reactive person (I'll explain later on about reactive people) who now has an excuse for their immature behaviours. This has got to be one of the biggest responsibility shirks of all time! I urge you not to buy into that theory, as, I don't know about you, but I can't really get my head around the idea that I have a naughty imp inside me, pulling my strings. I have visions of people in small groups sitting around in a circle, nodding and agreeing with the "therapist" when he sympathetically tells them "It's not your fault, it's the naughty child inside you that hasn't grown up yet". This would be a great joke if it weren't so sad. The fact is that the person who buys into this theory never learns to take responsibility for themselves as they are told that it isn't really them but the inner child who dictates them that is to blame. What a cop out!

Accept the fact that who you are and what you are doing are so because of the decisions and choices that you have made in your life. This is often the first step in beginning to access your true power. You cannot do that if you don't first grow up. As I said before, growing up has nothing to do with getting old — that is a different kettle of fish altogether. Growing up is saying that you are leaving all your old, silly behaviours behind so that you are now ready to live your life the way it was supposed to be lived. With passion, vigour and to the full!

Do not be afraid to take this leap; be afraid of staying the same. When you move away from old, negative behaviours you are opening yourself up to a life of joy and inner peace.

Don't make excuses

Whenever a client comes to see me I take down some details so that I can assess their needs. On the questionnaire the final question I ask is "Are you committed to doing whatever it takes" and 99% of those people state confidently a resounding "Yes". **Then** we get to the nitty gritty of what they need to do in order to solve their dilemma and cracks begin to appear. Often when the reality of what they have to do in order to help themselves is laid out in front of them they begin to put up barriers which would prevent progress. These barriers are not physical ones though but they are in fact **mental excuses**. Excuses that they try to use to get out of doing whatever is suggested to them. I've heard them all and I find that people can defend they're excuses quite powerfully with the reasons why they cannot fulfil a necessary plan of action. When a client complains that he / she is overweight and wants to lose it and I tell them that they need to join a health club they will often throw up about twenty shabby reasons why they cannot do just that. These reasons though are just **excuses** which when properly challenged even sound ridiculous to the person giving them! Things like I can't join a health club because I am not fit enough (as if avoiding it is going to improve the situation), or I will feel too self conscious around those toned fit people is another one that overweight people use. Think about yourself do you make excuses in life? Do you create mental barriers to convince yourself that you cannot or should not do something when you know you should? Do you blame lack of time for not being able to do something even though you waste time thinking of excuses to get out of it. If so it's time to stop making excuses for failings in your life and you must begin to abolish this weak mindset. Abolishing excuses from your life is another great step in taking full responsibility for your life and will create the foundations for the other principles outlined in this book. No longer seek to find excuses to get you off the hook as when you do you only sink deeper into the mire. People use excuses as the time to convince themselves into believing that there are reasons out of their control for not doing something or approaching something half heartedly. It's not enough to do that as you are only cheating yourself if you do. If you have done your very best and you simply could not do any more then that's OK but ask yourself the question "Did I really do my best?" and be honest with yourself.

Most people believe that the circumstances of their lives are what determine how they feel. Every week I hear people explain to me how they cannot control their emotions and actions and it is the circumstances in their lives that are to blame. If it **were** the circumstances that were to blame then every person when faced with the same set of circumstances would react in the same way — but they don't. To blame the circumstance for our own reactions and feelings is the mother of all shirking of responsibility! People tell me all the time that it was the shopping mall that made them uptight or that they couldn't find a parking space and it was those circumstances that are responsible for making them feel depressed and not themselves. To them it is not the fact that they reacted in such a stupid, immature way and worked themselves up; it was the other "causes" that did it to them. It is our **behaviour** that gets us worked up and not the circumstances in which we find ourselves. If you are truly going to live the best life ever, you have to stop acting and thinking as a victim of circumstances or whatever has happened in your past and decide to put **closure** on it. Yes, you didn't like it; O.K., it shouldn't have happened but it did and all the mental replaying of events will not change it and neither will asking **"WHY?"!** It just did — that's it! There is nothing more to analyse, and going through it over and over again will only bring about physical pain and unhappiness. It's time to get off that track and this is how we do it. We say:

"I didn't like those things that happened back then in my past, but today is <u>not then</u>; today is not the past; and I am not the past. I am ME. I can't change the past but I can change the course of MY future. So today I have decided to leave the past in the past, to let go of this heavy sack called 'my baggage from the past' and move on to a better life with a new beginning. No longer will I dwell on the negatives from the past because I have decided it ends NOW!"

One of the great pieces of advice I heard Anthony Robbins say was: "It's not change that takes time … it's the getting ready to change that takes time!" This is very true. When you make a decision — a true decision — then it's easy. No umming or erring or "maybes", though; it has to be a definite decision, a final decision, or it's worth nothing. That means no going back from your new decisions. Otherwise it won't stick; you have to use your **emotions** with your decisions for you to really make a change in yourself. You must have good reasons **why** you want to change first. You must decide whether you **want** to move away from the past, and finally decide what will happen if you don't change, versus what will happen if you do. Think of an issue that you want to change, that maybe you haven't been able to change, then run through the above steps to see if the answer is becoming clearer. Work out the pros and cons.

Then MAKE A DECISION.

<u>Changing Patterns of Behaviour</u>

There are times when wanting to change is not enough for the change actually to take place. This is especially true for behaviours such as phobias and compulsive behaviours, which have become habitual. Good intention is not enough to change a bad habit; nor is positive thinking usually enough to make a permanent change either. If, for instance, you are habitually unfaithful to your partner, although you hate the fact that you cause your loved one so much pain, by doing so you still feel compelled to do it again because it is a conditioned response. All the willpower and self-talk hasn't worked and whenever you go out you just go into your usual unfaithful mode. Even though you hate the rows and all the family upset it causes, it's still not enough to make you change your ways. The reason why is that, as bad as the consequences are for you, the "buzz" or feeling of pleasure associated with doing it is conditioned into your body as a feeling of pleasure. As long as that pleasure rush is there at the thought of being unfaithful, you will always have a battle to resist it. Somewhere in your past — maybe when you were single and quite sexually active — you became addicted to the rush of having lots of sexual partners. The challenge is that now, even though you are in a stable relationship, the old craving for sexual partners is still present. The need to do it is as strong as that of the smoker needing a cigarette. The reason that you have not been able to stop doing it is because you must change the feelings associated with it as well as having the right reasons to stop doing it. This change of associated feelings is what we are going to learn about next. We must break the pattern of feelings with a new set of feelings and condition them as a habit. This is how we do it.

Changing Bad Habits Exercise

1. Think about the bad habit that you don't want any more and recall the consequences in the **past** of having the habit. As vividly as you can, think about the embarrassment and shame that you have felt from having this habit. Remember incidents where it caused you anguish and at the same time begin to nip some part of your body so that it hurts. Keep on thinking about these past negative times with this bad habit and continue to nip parts of your body so that there is not just emotional pain but also physical pain at the thought of exercising this habit. Do this in different areas of your body. If one area seems to be getting used to it, you can also bend your fingers back at the same time as you visualise these past negative events. Do not hold back with this — with either the visualisation or the pain — as the more and the longer that you do it, the more it begins to de-condition your habit. Do this for about five minutes.

2. Now think about how this habit is destroying your **present life**. Think about how it is affecting you now and continue the pain procedure outlined in Step 1. Think about the anguish that the habit is causing in your life now and how you are messing things up for yourself by exercising it. Really start to make the thoughts and feelings powerful because the more powerful and dramatic they are, the more effective this procedure will be. How bad is your life now, with this habit? Start to make some pain somewhere in your body, maybe by nipping the skin on your hand. Keep nipping yourself at the thought of having this habit or negative behaviour in your life. Do this for five minutes too.

3. Now think about the consequences in the **future** of having this habit or behaviour and imagine what your life would be like if you still had it. Think about the misery of keeping this habit or behaviour forever and the impact that it will have in your life. Really focus on the negative consequences of what **will happen** if you don't change your ways and start to nip some area of your body at the same time. Really imagine the worst scenarios of keeping this behaviour and seeing it through to old age. Keep the pain going at the same time as thinking the horrendous thoughts as your mind and body are now starting to erase any feelings of pleasure that were once associated with the behaviour and replacing them with displeasure and revulsion. This should take another five minutes to do. At this point, if you have done the exercise properly, with 100 per cent effort and determination, the idea of doing the habit or behaviour ever again will be totally out of the question.

4.You probably feel physically and mentally exhausted at this point, so it's time to give yourself some good feelings. Let yourself become relaxed and begin to visualise your life now, without the old habit, and begin to see yourself acting and behaving in a whole new way in the situations where you used to have the old behaviour. Run this visualisation through for about five minutes to allow your inner mind to see the new way forward for you.

N.B. It is useful to continue the nipping exercise for about a month whenever a thought about the old habit comes to mind. However, do not cause yourself any physical harm by using this method and any "pain" should not continue after the exercise is completed. This is a very powerful technique but the idea is **not** to cause yourself any physical injury. Don't overdo it.

A change in your behaviour is just one good decision away.

The learning curve

One of the things that I run into all the time when I work with my personal clients is their inability to allow themselves to learn from their mistakes. So many times we don't allow ourselves the right to make errors in life and then over-criticise ourselves when we do, as if it should not be allowed! It's almost as if there is an **ideal** of ourselves, that we have to be perfect, that we can't make any errors in life and that if we do then there must be something wrong with us. This mindset still immobilises many people. This is not a healthy way of running our minds. This pedestal that we put ourselves on is often so ridiculously high that it is impossible to achieve. The fact that we can't attain it but we still think we should leads to a life of constant struggle and disappointment. We've got to bring this false ideal down to reality so that we can stop being disappointed and critical of ourselves. This doesn't mean that you shouldn't have high standards for yourself, though. What it does mean is that you now have a more realistic set of goals for yourself, that you can achieve.

Quite often, when I speak to people who complain that their lives are frustrating it is usually because they have so much on their plates that is impossible to do everything that they expect of themselves. Even if they could do it all, they would probably add more things on as time went by. The thinking that we can do everything we need to do every day and should always achieve it every day from then on is totally unrealistic. Even the most successful time management experts can't do everything they want to do **all of the time**. We all have times when we don't hit the mark; it's just a part of being human.

Make mistakes and grow stronger. Take that knowledge and create a wiser existence for yourself.

Also, hoping and wishing that other people should hit our ridiculously high mark is another error in thinking that causes so much frustration and unhappiness. The idea that we know best for our family and friends is nothing more than us **thinking** we know what is best (sometimes just for us) and then trying to control something that cannot be controlled. Rather than allowing somebody to live their own life and learn from their own mistakes, just as we did, we try to "guide" them into the right direction that **we think** is the right way.

Don't get me wrong; I am all for positive guidance but a lot of people I have met and worked with secretly try to mould their children or partners into something they believe is the ideal person, without really considering whether it is for the good of that person or not, sometimes just to show off to their friends that they are the "boss" of the relationship. How many times do couples break up when the more dominant personality tries to change the other person into their perceived ideal? When the partner does change the person is still not happy and can always find new faults with the partner until the partner's spirit and self-esteem are broken. Eventually the couple break up and the reason is that "You're not the person that I first met". Rarely do happy relationships last in such cases as at some point the underdog will suddenly snap and leave! I've seen mothers and fathers try to push their kids into careers that they don't want to be in; this can really break up families. I've seen kids pushed into behaving in certain ways and told what to read suddenly flip and go in the completely opposite direction. I've seen kids dye their hair red and cover themselves in tattoos and body piercing when parents try to manipulate them. I've even seen church-going kids turn into devil worshippers, and that **is** scary!

Know this:

YOUR KIDS ARE NOT YOU AND WILL NEVER BE YOU. THEY WILL NOT LIVE THE LIFE YOU WANTED FOR YOURSELF AND SHOULD NOT BE PUSHED INTO THINGS THAT DO NOT INTEREST THEM.

This doesn't mean that you shouldn't positively encourage them to succeed in their lives; just the opposite. Instead tell them:

"You can be whatever you want to be"

The latter statement is what you should say, and this is true. All through time there have been people who have had marvellous lives despite some dreadful starts —some born blind, some physically handicapped, others with crippling diseases — but somehow these people succeeded when many able-bodied people would have thrown in the towel. I never fail to be moved by the courage and determination of the para-Olympians who never moan or whine about the situations they are in; on the contrary, they see these things as merely challenges to conquer and they do it with determination on their faces. They have truly conquered the mind game.

I don't know of any successful and happy person who does not allow this very simple truth: that it is O.K., if not vital, for us to make mistakes in life. When we are kids it's accepted that we have to make mistakes and it is encouraged, such as when we learn to walk, but as adults we act like it's a sin. You have to fall down first of all in order for you to learn balance; it's also O.K. as an adult. In fact some businesses actually encourage it as they see this as a step forward on the road to progress.

One of the great stories that demonstrates this principle is the story the late Napoleon Hill tells in *Think and Grow Rich* when speaking to Thomas Edison who invented the electric lightbulb. After making over 10,000 attempts before succeeding in his dream, Edison told Hill:

"You know, I had to succeed, because I finally ran out of things that wouldn't work".

So if it's O.K. for history's geniuses to make mistakes then it's O.K. for us to do so too. What isn't O.K. is making the same mistake over and over again; then you're not learning. Say ***"What can I learn from this?"*** when mistakes occur — if you get hurt in a relationship, or you get angry about having to queue, or if you don't like the way you behaved towards your child, or you failed an exam. This simple phrase will engage your subconscious wisdom to come up with the appropriate answer. I never fail to be amazed by just how powerful this little technique is. Successful people know that success is a poor teacher. Learning comes from making mistakes. Listed next are some examples of solutions that often come into your awareness when you ask yourself the right questions.

- **I need to study harder**
- **I have to be more tolerant**
- **I need to practise a new behaviour**
- **I need to relax more**
- **I need to be less judgmental and more empathetic**
- **I have to be less self-centred**
- **I have to lower my "over the top" expectations**
- **I need to develop more self-confidence**
- **I need to choose my partners more carefully**
- **I need to stop smoking**
- **I need to eat better**
- **I need to go to the gym.**

These are some of the examples which the subconscious wisdom of your inner intelligence may tell you.

The opposite of the proactive person is the reactive. These people blame everybody and everything for their "bad luck" and always have a rehearsed excuse for why they can't succeed in life: "Oh, it's the people at work, they're idiots" or "So and so is just a lucky person — the gods smile on him!" or "It's not me, it's the rest of the world that's the problem!" or "It's the area I live in, there are no jobs here". These are just some examples of how reactive people try to shift responsibility from themselves and on to other people or things. Take health, for instance; where I live in the U.K. we have a National Health Service so that, if you get sick, you get free health care. You hear grossly overweight people moaning that the wait for treatment is too long as they puff on another cigarette and munch through another burger! Recently I heard a guy complaining that his new knee joint wasn't working well enough and wasn't healing fast enough; he then blamed the incompetence of the doctors, but this guy weighed in excess of 300 pounds! Whose responsibility is our health? Is it ours, or is it the doctor's?

To take full responsibility for yourself is to gain the ultimate power over your life.

There is so much information available to us now regarding our health, through the Internet and other free resources, that it's ridiculous to pretend that we don't know the dangers of smoking. Also recently, I heard another guy complaining that the drugs his wife was taking for the blocked artery disease she had weren't working properly, even though she was still smoking in the very hospital that was trying to help her!

These, and many other, examples of not wanting to take responsibility for our own health are what causes the waiting lists to be so long in the first place. It is one thing to go to hospital for something over which you have no control but it is another to need to go in because of ignorance and neglect of your health. Take charge of yourself now and start to take full responsibility for your health: I promise: you won't regret it.

Without our health we cannot enjoy the fruits of our labours.

You are responsible for:

- **your weight**
- **your happiness**
- **your relationships**
- **your salary**
- **your health**
- **your strength**
- **your intelligence**
- **your behaviours**
- **your job satisfaction**
- **your whole life.**

Nobody can do it for you!

Regardless of whether you like it or not, you are responsible for all the above circumstances; the sooner you believe that and accept this fact, the sooner you will begin to take control of your life.

A proactive person is a good planner, somebody who knows the purpose of his or her actions and will not be deterred if things aren't going to plan. Take the story of Bill and Tony. Both work in the steel industry, doing the same job. For a few years now the company that they both work for has been laying people off more and more and all the signs are pointing towards future closure. Tony is proactive and senses that this is going to happen. Knowing that his skills are limited to this industry, he embarks on a night course in I.T. and computer programming; he also decides to start developing his communication skills with some great personal development tapes. Soon he has "Plan B" fully up and running and is earning more than he did before, always looking for new ways to develop his knowledge and skills for the future. He is aware that to survive in the game of life **you have to be ahead of it**, so he is always looking for new niches and opportunities to improve his skills.

Bill, on the other hand, got all depressed and became very angry with the "system", waiting for the eventual closure and redundancy. He bought a new car and went on holiday with his family, blowing all his redundancy pay. Now, with the belief that "there are no jobs" firmly fixed in his mind, he spends his time sitting in the pub, moaning about the government and the injustice of it all. He picks up his morning newspaper and reads about another football player getting another pay rise to his already fantastic wages, and gets even more bitter and angry. Soon his home life is a ball of negativity and his wife leaves him (which is also the fault of the government). He spends the rest of his life moaning and looking for excuses for his unemployment while finding little ways to scam the government!

This short story shows two people in the same situation, but with two different outcomes. Which one would you be? The moaner, or the mover?

When we moan about our life and then do nothing then we do not have the right to moan.

One of the problems that people often come to see me about is their inability not only not to learn from the past but also not to move away from it; to live continually as if whatever occurred in the past is always going to be around to haunt them or recur in the future. This is a very common negative thought process that promotes only misery and is also **not true**. One of the principles that prevents this negative scenario has been discussed already: if you don't learn from your mistakes, you will be condemned to re-live them.

Understand this:

"The past does not equal the future"

Anthony Robbins

Just because things happen in the past, it doesn't meant that these things automatically then have to recur in the future. We are not robots, we are not pre-programmed, we are free-thinking individuals with the ability to choose our responses and actions. We are the only creatures on Earth who can do that; all God's other creatures can only act on their instinct — we have **choice**. If we didn't then you would never have learned to walk. You would have tried and then fallen over and said to yourself: "Well, that's it, I just can't do it" and then resigned yourself to a life without mobility. But no, you tried again and then again until you walked because, as a baby, you hadn't learned about self-criticism yet (unlike us adults!). We use the past as the constant reference point whenever we think about doing something in the future. This is understandable, as what else do we have? It is true that we need these memories to help guide us through our decision-making but how many times do we chicken out of doing something just because when we were younger and less experienced we tried something and didn't succeed? Proactive people understand that there is no failure — only feedback and opportunities to learn. You **must** begin to think in the same way if a happy, successful life is what you desire.

Accept mistakes as an essential part of life; they are the yardsticks to a better future.

Take the example of David. David was a 17-year-old young man going for his first real job interview. Nervous and unprepared, David really got flustered and was lost for words when the time for the interview came. He blushed and was nearly sick by the time it had finished. Now, five years on and five years wiser, his confidence has increased ten-fold. Then a promotion comes up and he has to attend an interview. All of a sudden the memories come flooding back to him about the time when he was 17 and all the old feelings return, and the beads of sweat start to show on his brow. David decides to reject the opportunity of the promotion and decides that he is safer doing his less mentally challenging position, convincing himself that the real reason he avoided the interview was that he didn't really fancy the job. Another young upstart with a different viewpoint on making mistakes goes for the interview and gets the job. This example happens many times the world over, and is a confidence-eroding process, because every time that you avoid something like this you are convincing yourself that this is something that you can't do. The other person who gets the job has come to understand that mistakes are just a natural part of growing up and that, as long as a person doesn't continue making the same mistakes time and time again, then that is O.K. This person reflects in a relaxed manner to extract the **learning** from an error in order to gain some new knowledge and understanding from it. Hence this person lives a life of greater inner peace and confidence.

Understand this: The person you are today does not have to be the person you are tomorrow; every day we are given the gift of a new day to wipe the slate clean, an opportunity for a fresh start and a new beginning. Why not embrace this powerful truth now and decide make a fresh start tomorrow?

I once read a great quote that said:

"Your ability or capability is not limited to your past experience. Your past defines what you have done … your capability defines what you could do. Be defined by your true capability and not your past experience!"

I think this sums it up pretty well.

Fate. Fact or fiction?

Not counting personal tragedies such as accidents and the like, do you believe in fate? Do you believe that who we are is determined at birth? Does God have different baskets for different people; some going into the "successful" basket, some into the "steady away" basket and the last basket is the "unlucky" basket? Do you think that something similar occurs and that is why, no matter what you do, you seem to have bad luck? Let's investigate this!

Are some people just lucky or do they work smarter?

This question will definitely get a "lucky" answer from the reactive thinker. They will say "I work hard but I don't get the same pay" which is probably true but working hard is one thing and working smart is another. I know of no successful person who does not only work hard but also plans and **makes** the openings happen for themselves. They do not sit and wait for luck to smile on them; instead they do whatever it takes to achieve their goals. You cannot become successful and do it totally on luck alone. While the reactive thinker sits in the pub and thinks "Why me?" the proactive person is out doing what it takes to become successful. The reactive person wants to believe in luck as it excuses them from actually becoming successful. So the answer is: no, they are not just lucky, they think smarter and work smarter. Having the right attitude to life and being a positive thinker cause their "luck" — nothing more, nothing less.

Do some people have a charmed life?

Why do some people always seem to fall on their feet, no matter what, while others seem to struggle all the time? It's all down to attitude. These people have the same problems as everybody else but **they** do not let them take over their lives, so the answer to this question is a simple **no**, they don't live a charmed life but they do think and operate on a different mindset to those who don't. These people react and think differently to those who get stressed and go to pieces every time something goes wrong. They do not over-react in testing situations and they let their wisdom guide them through whatever it is they need to do without the need to become over-dramatic about things. Their positive attitude is the driving force for the positive results they receive ("You only get out what you put in"). The negative mindset is like a magnet as it attracts negative things.

Do fortune-tellers know the answer?

Unless the fortune-teller is a massively successful person, I would never look for advice from them. This route is yet again the favourite of the person who wants to believe in unseen forces determining our lives. This is the ultimate in shifting personal responsibility. Do not fall into the trap of wanting to see such people for guidance; instead, put your faith in yourself and your God if you believe in one. The person who seeks reassurance from "mystic" means is almost certainly a conscious mind thinker. Something happens to people who crave these means for daily guidance: **nothing**. Nothing ever happens because they are always waiting for it to happen rather than getting out there and making it happen!

Does what goes around really come around?

In my experience, **yes** it does, as long as your intention is genuine and there is no hidden motive involved. The phrase "You reap what you sow" is a typical example of such a phenomenon. Whenever people do bad things in their lives for a time they **seem** to get away with it. Sometimes they get away with it for years until they get hit with the big one. I've seen drug dealers swan around in expensive cars as if they are untouchable for years, until their luck runs out and they end up in jail. I try to be polite to every person I meet, even if that person isn't always polite back to me. The key is to be polite for no other reason other than it's nice to be so. Do not expect or want other people to be the same. If you hold a door open for somebody, do not complain if they don't say "Thank you". Do not set that condition up in your mind beforehand so that you will be annoyed if they don't say "Thank you". Do not be polite to receive gratification; do it as a matter of course. Do it because it's a nice thing to do. If a shop assistant does not say "Thank you" for your business, have the mindset that you don't **need** for them to be polite in order for you to enjoy your day. If a waiter is a little "off" with you, don't get all annoyed about it; just let it go and accept it as a part of life. This mindset brings about a real feeling of inner peace. Not wanting and needing someone to act or behave in the ways that you expect them to stops the feelings of anger and disappointment when they go against that expectation. If you **do** get angry with impolite people, you are then allowing their actions to influence your feelings, which takes away your self-power. If you react negatively to somebody, they are controlling you. Not reacting strengthens your self-power. I see people all the time who get angry when the people they meet don't match their expectations of how they should behave or be. The fact is that it is **we** who need to change and not them. We must lower our own expectations to the more realistic truth; that it is the way of the world that not every person we meet will be polite to us. Truly absorbing this fact is a large step towards greater peace. When you don't expect it, you won't be disappointed when it doesn't happen.

You find that the most successful people in the world are not only takers but are givers too. The people who only take usually befit some kind of personal tragedy, which nobody cares about when it happens. The more good you give out, the more good you will receive but do it because it's the right thing to do and not for what you can get.

The truth about fate is that although things happen to us, which seem to test our resolve at times, we all have the choice about how to react when they do. I believe we all have a plan, a course that we should follow, that in some way helps to bring about a worldwide difference. The problem is, though, most of us are so bogged down with our own thoughts and problems that the path is never actualised. Do not leave things up to fate; instead begin now to take another big step in fulfilling your destiny, and move on to Chapter 2!

Chapter Two

Principle 2: Your Thoughts Control Your Feelings

The difference between highly successful people and those who only aspire to the average — in a nutshell.

Through studying people throughout my adult life, I have come to some startling findings with regard to the different mindsets of the two types of people that we encounter: the super-successful and those who are averagely successful. Less than 5 per cent of the world's population actually goes beyond the success level of the average person and into the realms of the super-successful. Most people (the other 95 per cent) are slightly above the average, become the average or are below the average in terms of success. So what separates these two personality types? The biggest difference I have found is that the super-successful people of the world are predominantly subconscious inner wisdom thinkers while the average person is predominantly a conscious mind thinker. What does that mean? Read on!

The conscious mind thinker rarely aspires to anything great because the conscious mind is always looking to find fault and criticise any thought, which it believes is too ambitious. Whenever an ambitious thought or idea is brought to mind (from the subconscious) it is immediately analysed and criticised until the conscious mind finds a fault. Soon, whatever the thought or idea is, is mentally pulled apart until it no longer seems sensible. This process of over-analysis is employed whenever a new thought or idea may take a conscious mind thinker outside the comfort zone. The conscious mind thinker takes these negative conscious mind doubts very seriously indeed and nine times out of ten "back heels" the idea. He or she uses this frustrating process all of their life and this is what keeps them from ever really taking the chances that actually might have yielded a better outcome. The conscious mind is always ready to dream up some negative scenarios to throw a spanner in the works on any new plan or idea. The more those doubts are accepted — whether they are personal doubts or perceptional ones — the more they become conditioned ways of thinking. For example, if a conscious mind thinker thinks about starting a new college course and becomes excited at the prospect of starting it, the conscious mind will usually try to sabotage the idea with negative input and scenarios to put them off. The doubts creep in.

Somebody who is heavily influenced by their conscious mind thoughts may abandon the idea now that they are "thinking about it realistically". For the conscious mind thinker there is always reason to doubt, always reasons to be wary and there is always a "But what if?" to watch out for. This sorry state of affairs is the reason that so many talented, able people never reach their true potential and instead live average lives. Why? Because they believed the negative chatter of the conscious mind instead.

On the other hand, the subconscious inner mind thinker has learned either automatically or through experience that the negative chatter of the conscious mind is not important and therefore is not to be taken too seriously. Instead of running with and analysing those negative thoughts they immediately dismiss them into the wastepaper bin in their mind and forget about them. Through experience the person has found this the best way to live or perhaps they have done this automatically. This thinker understands the power of thoughts and rather than using them to destroy their potential they use them wisely, to propel themselves into success. They understand that there is no practical benefit in thinking such ridiculous thoughts, so they don't do it. The subconscious inner mind thinker is a cool customer and remains so when others are getting stressed. They are able calmly to think through the best options for solving problems and are able to make good judgements because of that. Self-belief is not something that such a person has to keep reinforcing in themselves as, without the chatter of the conscious mind, their thinking is clear and knowing anyway. No self-bolstering is needed for the inner subconscious thinker as they are wisdom thought-driven. Fault-finding and self-criticism are not wise either so they do not play any part of the daily routine for this person.

Without the constant annoying chatter of the conscious mind to bother them, the subconscious inner wisdom thinker is very goal-oriented and looks forward to taking on new ventures. Whether they be new career directions, new hobbies or anything which excites and gets the juices going, such a thinker never questions whether they can do it or not.

Failure to succeed never comes into the equation as this person has total faith in their inner wisdom to guide them. When things happen in life that some people may call "negative" the subconscious inner mind thinker looks at solving the problem rather than focusing on the problem itself. Thinking that every challenge that life throws at us is a lesson from which we can understand and grow wiser from is another characteristic of such a thinker. This thinker typically makes good decisions and can be perceived as "lucky" by some people who have the majority mindset. They do not take seriously the negative doom and gloom of the conscious mind so they remain unaffected by it.

So there you have it I know this is going to be a difficult decision but which part of your mind are you going to use for your life? Let me show you how to begin to take this knowledge and start to change the way you think and live forever!

To run your life by the conscious mind is like taking a Rolls Royce to a stock car rally.

The goal of this chapter is to help you to begin to make the switch from using your conscious mind to run your life to that of using your subconscious mind instead. When you do this you begin to gain the total control of your mind as your thoughts control your feelings. Of all the principles outlined in this book, understanding that your thoughts control your feelings is the **biggest** factor in maintaining your mental health and overall happiness. Truly understanding the following information is the key to controlling the way you feel. Understanding and using the true power of your own thoughts can eliminate all unwanted emotions such as anger, depression, stress, fear and lack of self-confidence. Let's face it: if you could control your emotions and nothing else you would live a fantastic life, wouldn't you? Imagine if you could do that, if you could have the same control over your mind as you do with your T.V. remote control. Is this possible, though? Surely not, our minds are just random thought-producing machines, aren't they? The answer is no, they are not. We are actually the conductors and controllers of our minds and knowing this is the first part of learning how to use it more effectively. Not knowing this fact leaves us at the mercy of our minds and whatever consequences happen after that. You **can** control your mind: you just have to know **how** to do it! Without the knowledge of how to do it you're always at the mercy of every negative thought that enters your mind. Negative thoughts can literally wreck every part of your life, including your friendships, your marriage and your working life. You must learn to have control of your thoughts. Let me show you how!

Whenever a client comes to see me I always tell them the same thing: there are two ways we can go about solving your problem. We can go down the traditional analytical road of therapy, where we go back through your past and try to find the root cause for your problem and why it started. Week after week we could relive old, painful memories of past events, get through the "repressed anger and pain", dredging through long-forgotten memories and opening old wounds until we find the "demon" at the core. After finally dragging it up from the depths of your mind and strangling it, we begin to delve a little more to see if there are any more hidden "issues" to keep us going for years to come. Or we can understand that it is **always** our **thoughts** that control how we feel and so instead teach ourselves how to learn to control our thoughts instead to move us in a more positive and productive state, to finally get along with enjoying life again. This is what I want to do with you. The analytical way is an extremely time-consuming plan of action which in my experience can often lead to more harm than good. Many analytical therapists still use this approach and I can only deduce that the client receiving such treatment must have plenty of money as well as patience. But don't get me wrong: I'm not knocking counselling — counsellors do a great job and in my experience are very caring and dedicated people. When we lose relatives or are victims of crime these people are invaluable in those early stages. Talking through things at this point can be very helpful for people who need it. What I'm talking about is long-term analytical therapy, which doesn't teach people to move from the past and into the present (here and now), helping people to gain confidence in themselves. The new idea of "self-awareness", or what I call self-analysis, is another way people stir up the faulty thought processes of the conscious mind.

What we need to do is to begin to stop using the conscious mind for such counter-productive means and start to use the subconscious wisdom instead. Many people who come to see me seeking help have been heavily into "self-awareness" and are now **totally aware** of their "problems and limitations", often without knowing they had them before! They are now able to remember negative things from the past that they had once forgotten, which now start to stir the negative analysis process again. Most of my clients are too acutely aware of their problems and are literally blowing them out of proportion with the process of **over-thinking**. The goal of this chapter is to get you thinking less about yourself and more about just enjoying your life! So going down the road of analysis is definitely not on the cards for us if we want to live the best life ever.

To analyse ourselves is to waste our precious time; to waste our precious time is abusing the gift of life.

Think of an issue that you have that for some time has been bothering you. Please pause and do this.

I'm going to make an assumption. You have analysed this problem until you are blue in the face, and what have you come up with?

Nothing!

(Nothing of any real value, anyway.)

Did going over and over the problem in your mind help you? What have you actually come up with in any real sense? Not a lot. The statements "Why did it happen?" or "I wish I could change the past" are the ones people tell me most often. Whenever people come to see me asking "Why me?" my answer is always the same: "Why anybody?".

You see, it's human nature to question why things happen: the problem with trying to figure it out using your conscious mind is that you will rarely come up with an answer making any sense! You will get lots of different crazy theories thrown at you within seconds, which is because the conscious mind is designed for quick thinking and not **wise** thinking. The conscious mind is always analysing and judging life but should not be used for inner reflection.

This is where the problems start. Whenever you let your conscious mind direct you, you live a life of over-caution and indecision. In the conscious mind there is **always** a reason to be wary, suspicious and alert! This can lead to stress and paranoia. Also, decisions are very hard to make because you have two voices in your head telling you two different things at the same time. Most people use the conscious mind to direct them in their lives, which is risky. To see whether you do, just see if the below questions ring a bell with you. Do these seem familiar? Please tick the ones that you can relate to:

- **You have an inability to make decisions**
- **You think people are talking about you**
- **You are a worrier**
- **You get stressed easily**
- **You feel depressed often**
- **You are very emotional**
- **You avoid new challenges**
- **You like soap operas**
- **You fear change**
- **You don't like planes/trains/cars**
- **You watch the news avidly**
- **You expect the worst**
- **You believe what people say (negative)**
- **You believe in bad luck/superstitions/tarot**
- **You don't like yourself.**

If you ticked less than five, you probably feel O.K. most of the time but you sometimes worry and feel down.

If you ticked between six and ten, you have a generally negative outlook on life. You are probably not the life and soul of the party and are not having a fantastic life, to say the least. You are a conscious mind thinker.

If you ticked more than ten, you really need to absorb and apply **every** bit of this information. You worry constantly and feel mentally and physically overloaded. You are **even more** of a conscious mind thinker.

Do you want to stay the same or do you want to change?
Congratulations! You have taken the brave and necessary decision to turn your life around. And there's no going back now: whatever you scored above, you can turn things around no matter how bad they are.

I've seen people in my office in tatters and in a few weeks of applying these principles totally transform themselves!

It can happen for **you**! It's not a question of "Will it work?": we are going to **make** it work. We will **make it happen!**

So we've determined that some work has to be done, and that's always the start of it. So, what can be done? Here is the **truth**.

The difference between happy and unhappy people is the thoughts they think. Nothing more.

Happy people have happy, positive-thinking thoughts and unhappy people have unhappy, negative-thinking thoughts. That's it!

Yes, this is the **truth**. Happy people either know naturally or have learned not to take their negative thoughts too seriously. They waft them away and don't pay too much attention to them, understanding that thoughts are just thoughts and that you don't have to think them if you don't want to. They understand that they have an inner wisdom, which can guide them if only they shut down the chatter of the conscious mind. They understand that believing and acting on the "chatter" of the conscious mind is a waste of time and counter-productive. Whenever they feel like they're getting a little stressed they stop what they're doing, take a breather and relax their minds. At that point they have full access to their wise inner mind, which is also known as the subconscious mind. They know that this is the place to ask the questions if problems arise.

The thoughts we think are what makes us either happy or sad, and not the circumstances in our lives.

Unhappy people, on the other hand, take their negative thoughts very seriously indeed. They run with them, believe them and because of that they live on adrenalin. To them, every thought must be re-thought and analysed to get to the "truth", which is usually some negative belief they have that has been reinforced with the repetition of the thought and some carefully selected examples to back it up! They live to be validated to be proved right in their thinking and usually will be at some time or another (if you go looking for something hard enough, you will find it). Then an even greater reference is born which solidifies with every negative repetition of the thought. Soon, everything is going wrong as they become more serious and all the time they are feeling worse and worse. You can't even crack a joke without them tutting at your "Stupid immaturity".

Depression is now prevalent and the world is to blame. People at work, customers, bosses, the government, the weather, their friends and family are the cause, **not** the negative-thinkers' thinking. Life is dull and positive thinking is for people out of touch with reality. Change of work scares negative thinkers, even though they hate their job, but they can always find an excuse to stay safe. Good old conscious mind is always there to help them see the hidden dangers of moving to a better job. That's in the unlikely event that anyone wants to hire them in the first place!

There is a big difference in the two different examples above but the main variation is in the different ways they feel. As the title of this principle says, your thoughts control your feelings. This simple statement cannot be underestimated in its power. What do I mean by "its power"? Another truth is that:

You cannot feel any emotion in your body without first thinking a thought.

That's right: you have to **think** first in order to feel. I'm not talking about physical symptoms, like indigestion or bloatedness, which are normal human complaints, I'm talking about emotional feelings such as anger, and stress, jealousy or depression — the list goes on. Try it: make yourself depressed without thinking first. You can't — it's impossible! This is great news, which means that if you've ever suffered from stress or depression in the past **you have caused it by YOUR OWN thinking**. That's right: you caused it yourself by the very thoughts you decided to think. This may seem a little harsh or maybe unbelievable but think about it. Your body cannot create feelings like these by itself: it has to get the stimulus from your brain to tell it what to feel. What you probably have not been aware of is that you were thinking those thoughts that produced the feelings in the first place. They happen so quickly that we don't realise that we think them; it's like **boom** and they're in, but the first we know about them is that we have an awful feeling. **Then** we think "Why?". Then the whole analysis thing starts again, causing more confusion and taxing the conscious mind, which holds little wisdom with regard to finding a sensible answer. Rarely does a sensible answer come to mind at this point unless, through the depths, the subconscious manages to find a way through to come to your aid.

Our thoughts are the driving force of our feelings and emotions so we must learn to use them wisely!

So, if our thoughts control our feelings, why do so many people turn to alcohol, food, cigarettes or drugs to help them feel better? The simple reason is this. Unless you fully understand the principle that **your thoughts control your feelings**, you may fall into the trap of looking for these external things to help change the way you feel which in time will cause a bigger problem than the ones that you are using them to help with!

PEOPLE WHO FIND THEY NEED THOSE EXTERNAL AIDS HAVE NOT MASTERED THEIR MINDS AND ARE PROBABLY NOT AWARE THAT THEY CAN BE MASTERED AS EASILY AS YOU ARE ABOUT TO LEARN RIGHT NOW!

That's right: most people are not aware that we have the ability to run our minds and gain total control of the way we feel. If we don't have the **knowledge** of what to do and how to do it, we will find something that works in the short term — like smoking. If, for example, whenever something difficult at work comes up or you encounter a challenging customer and you feel wound up, and you light a cigarette you are probably using the only way you know to deal with the situation at that time. If you don't know what else to do, you will automatically reach for the cigarette regardless of the fact that you know how many people die from smoking-related diseases every year. It's the instant fix. It does have some kind of positive benefit at the time, otherwise you wouldn't do it. If that's all you know, that's all you can do!

The same goes for food; if you have a tough day and you work hard or you feel depressed, you can reward yourself with your favourite food. And lots of it! But, and I mean but, these "cures" are just temporary means that, in time, will prove to be an even bigger problem. Because if you smoke, in time the little nagging voice in your head that tells you that you'd better stop will get louder and louder as you yet again hear of somebody else who has died prematurely due to smoking. Even trying to convince yourself that you are not bothered by it becomes even more difficult as your body starts to feel the corrosive effects of the cigarettes. Thoughts of hospitals and hideous operations come into your awareness more and more, as you try to banish them from your mind. Even switching over the channel on your T.V. in an effort to hide from the reality of what could be you, whenever an anti-smoking commercial comes on doesn't work any more. Or, as the weight of all the food you have been medicating yourself on becomes your enemy, as you now cannot stand the person you see in the mirror, so you eat to ease the pain. And the cycle starts again next day.

When the conscious mind is allowed to rule, we take the consequences of this error, which are usually grave.

This goes for any behaviour, both physically or mentally, that people use to "help" the situation. For every behaviour that we have there is a **payoff** — something you get out of it, otherwise you wouldn't do it. For example, I once had a teenage girl who came to see me because every time she went to school she needed to go to the toilet three or four times a lesson. This had become so bad that her parents had her leave the school for the time being and had her personally tutored. Every medical test had been done and no physical problem could be found. She was a very friendly and intelligent girl but people often took advantage of this at school. When I asked her what the **payoff** for the problem was, she said there wasn't one. She finally admitted that "one good thing" was that she didn't have to go to school and face the people who gave her a hard time.

It's like the subconscious coming up with a solution for avoiding these people, which at one level worked but at another level failed. The girl wanted to avoid school but she didn't like the embarrassment of needing the toilet all the time! So this is what I mean: if you don't know what to do instead, then who knows what you might come up with? People use external aids such as smoking to try to block out the pain of their own thoughts.

Then there's the story of the guy who couldn't get his work out of his mind so he drank himself to sleep every night to try to shut it off (payoff). But then he lost his job because he couldn't function effectively next day and became obnoxious with his clients. Or the lady who was devastated when her husband ran off with his secretary and left her with the kids, so then she turned to eating and gained 200 pounds so that "no man would ever find me attractive and hurt me again". But she found that, because of her weight, she could no longer function in the ways that she wanted and could not partake in any fun days out with her kids.

So how can we solve this problem?

These people, and other people who use the same coping strategies to try to solve their problems, do it for one reason. They weren't aware that they had other **choices** available to them. They only knew one choice. There are always millions of different choices we can make when faced with challenges but we tend to have tunnel vision and do what we've always done out of **habit.** If you think you have no choice, then you only go for the choice you know at the time! So what's my point? Well, this is why I devised these principles: to give you lots of different choices. I'm giving you different choices of how to think, different choices of how to view the world, and different choices of how to live your life. You see, we can only make new choices if we have more information to have as a resource to help us.

There is always more than one choice but we can only begin to see them when we look in different directions.

With all of the common problems that were discussed briefly above, there were plenty of alternatives that could have been used instead, now that we know that we do have lots of other choices. There is so much information around these days: with the boom of the Internet, information that would never have been generally known to us or might have been restricted to the medical world is now right in front of us —

right in our homes. Once you go looking, it's amazing what you can find. It's like when you buy a new car and then suddenly realise how many cars of the same make and model as yours are on the road. Suddenly, because you are looking for them, you see them all the time!

When you ask the question "How can I?", rather than "Why?" then you are asking the right questions for solving your problems. Let's take the example of stress, which is a common problem. If you ask the question "Why do I feel this way?" this prompts your conscious mind to go looking for reasons. You may come up with twenty or so different reasons for the stress and as you think about each one you feel yourself getting more and more stressed. Suddenly your body has adrenalin pumping through your veins and your good judgement has gone out of the window. Now you are consumed with an overwhelming feeling of anxiety and information overload. Before a question is answered, another one pops in, making it even more difficult to make sense of it all. At this point you are desperate for it to stop, so you think of something that in the past has helped you cope in similar situations, so you go for the quick fix: alcohol, drugs, or whatever. In the short term this gives some relief! But if the same thoughts arise next day, the whole thing starts over again like an endless loop.

There is another way

If you ask the question "How can I?" instead of "Why?", this is a question which is then directed to the wisdom of your subconscious mind. Instead of taxing the conscious mind, with its very limited resources, you are now asking the part of the mind with all the knowledge and information you have ever learned from the day you were born to the age you are now, for its wisdom. The conscious mind can only concentrate on something like seven things at once! Compare that with the capacity of the subconscious, which is just about infinite. So it makes sense to use the resources of your inner subconscious mind, and not the limited conscious mind, to help you make the right decisions. This is what **all** successful people do.

If success is your aim it will not come by being a conscious mind thinker; to join the ranks of the successful you must trust your inner wisdom.

I know what you're thinking: this is all good and well but what does that really mean and how can I start to use this process? There are many ways to use the subconscious mind to help you. The first thing you need to know is how to distinguish the subconscious wisdom and the conscious mind chatter. Here's the answer: when you ask the subconscious mind for assistance the answer should come back to you in a relaxed, wise-sounding manner. It will have a common-sense feel to it, it will seem wise and it will make obvious sense. It may seem so obvious that you may have known it deep down anyway, but denied it as you continued to listen to the conscious mind chatter. Quite often the answer is not as "earth shattering" as you might have thought, just plain old common sense. It may come through immediately or it may take an hour, a day or a few days. It could come through as words (talking speech) or a picture or maybe just a feeling or inner knowing. The key is not to try to force it because if you do and you become stressed, the conscious mind will come into play and mess things up. Once you're using your conscious mind again, you could fall into the trap of believing that "this issue" really is a big issue that should be analysed and scrutinised, and the whole thing starts again! The conscious mind will make you wound up and it may have an "emergency" feel about it, but don't trust it as it's not coming from your wisdom.

Wisdom is the gut instinct that you knew was there all the time, telling you the right thing to do. Never ignore it.

O.K., so how do I begin to gain access to the wisdom of the subconscious mind?

There are lots of different ways in which people have been gaining access to and using the power of the wise inner mind. There is meditation, self-hypnosis, crystals, praying and countless other ways to do it. All can work and lots of people use the above methods, and that's great. If you find a way that suits you and you get great results, then all power to you. If you're like me, though, time is precious and I like to do things simply and quickly, so this is how I do it.

I find a quiet place by myself, close my eyes and take a few deep, relaxing breaths. After about 30 seconds I ask a question to my subconscious mind, something like:

"What do I need to do in order to solve the X problem?"
or
"Why do I feel this way?"
or
"What else can I do to make things better with person X?"

Then I just wait there, staying relaxed. I don't try to force an answer but I usually get one within seconds as I now have a very good relationship with my inner mind. It is vital that you give 100 per cent trust to your inner mind and don't ask too many questions at once. Also, I am always very respectful when asking questions and always say "thank you" whatever the answer. Listed below are some examples of things that you may want to ask your wise inner mind. You may want to change them a little bit to reflect your circumstances:

"What can I do to stop this stress?"
"Why do I have this behaviour and what is my payoff?"
"What do I have to do in order to lose weight?"
"How can I improve my relationships?"
"How is my health?"
"What do I have to do in order to change my life?"
" What do I have to do, to really succeed at X?"
"I need to move on, will you help me?"
"Is my partner the right one for me?"
"Why do I get these headaches?"
"What do I have to do in order to be a great parent?"
"Is this the right job for me?"
"How can I change my behaviour?"

That's it. That's all you have to do. Ask the right specific questions and you will receive the proper answers. You must have total trust in your inner mind's ability to serve you though, and soon you will become aware of an inner guidance that will be with you at all times. You might call it a gut instinct or just an inner knowing but as you trust it more and more you will find yourself thinking clearer than you've ever done before!

Getting a better answer is just a case of asking a better question and knowing to which mind to direct it.

But what about the chatter?

There's a great analogy that is used in Richard Carlson's brilliant book *Stop Thinking and Start Living* which describes the conscious mind's chatter as "static" interference in your mind that grows with attention. What this means is that the conscious mind chatter is nothing more than background hiss that shouldn't be taken so seriously. Whenever you do, you run the risk of unwise advice and stressful times ahead. So the key to inner peace, then, is not to be over-run with the conscious mind chattering. Your ability to **dismiss** the conscious mind chatter is the key to happiness and success in your life.

O.K., so how do we do that?

Well, this part is easy, but it does take a bit of practising on our part to make it work effectively. The good news is that it is something that you already do now, without knowing it. That is because your subconscious mind does it for you so that you can go through your day without being bothered. It has been estimated that we have approximately 50,000 thoughts per day, and that's a lot of thoughts! If you had to sit there and think all of those thoughts one at a time you wouldn't even get out of bed in the morning because, as soon as you were going to get up, another thought would pop into your mind, and then you would have to think it and so on. You would never get any thing done, so thankfully there is another part of the mind that takes care of them for you, and ,yes, you guessed it: it's the subconscious mind.

The subconscious is also the part of the mind that helps you breathe, tells you when to blink and regulates your blood pressure, so you can be sure that it is truly wise. Of all those 50,000 thoughts we have, I reckon about 45,000 of them are just garbage thinking and float in and out of your mind waiting to be dropped into the mental garbage can in your subconscious mind's abyss. These are just the random thoughts that come and go all day long and usually recur most days without our really noticing them. They do not have large emotional charges connected to them or, if they do, we forget them quickly. Thought example: "I'll have to vacuum the car later" (or something mundane like that). These thoughts are automatically wafted away by the subconscious mind and disposed of into your mental garbage can automatically for you. But the process is **not perfect**: the subconscious mind can often let silly, negative thoughts slip though the net. If these thoughts get through and are taken seriously they will wind you up. These thoughts are the chatter that should have been dismissed but, because you have run with them, analysed them and taken them seriously, they now control the way you feel. If these types of thoughts are allowed to come into your daily thinking repeatedly they will gain strength and start to carve your personality for you. Now if these thoughts were positive thoughts, then things would be great and you would start to carve a positive life with positive outcomes.

Your subconscious mind is the best friend that you have: respect it and cherish the service it provides.

But if these thoughts are of a negative manner, they are very destructive to your mental and physical health, culminating in the symptoms known as stress or depression. If these thoughts are repeated enough (approximately every day for a month) they them become a habit, which then occurs automatically. The first step to recovery is to acknowledge that you need to do something about it. The second step is to expect and know that these negative thoughts **will** try to pop into your thinking, so be ready for them.

When you are aware of a negative thought that has popped into your awareness you are now faced with a choice: do I **accept** it or do I **reject** it? (Bearing in mind what the consequences will be if you accept a negative thought.) When negative thoughts pop into your mind, you are at a **crossroads** where a choice has to be made. Which way you decide to go — **acceptance** or **rejection** — will determine the way you will feel afterwards. So, given that choice, you can think about it this way: Ask yourself:
"When I have thought this thought in the past, did it take me towards a positive outcome?"

If it didn't, you have the choice of whether you want to keep it or not. This is simple, really, when you think of it in these terms: there are only two options — yes or no!

The first step in gaining control of your life is to gain control of your mind.

Please study the diagram below which will show you what I am talking about.

The "thought crossroads" scenario

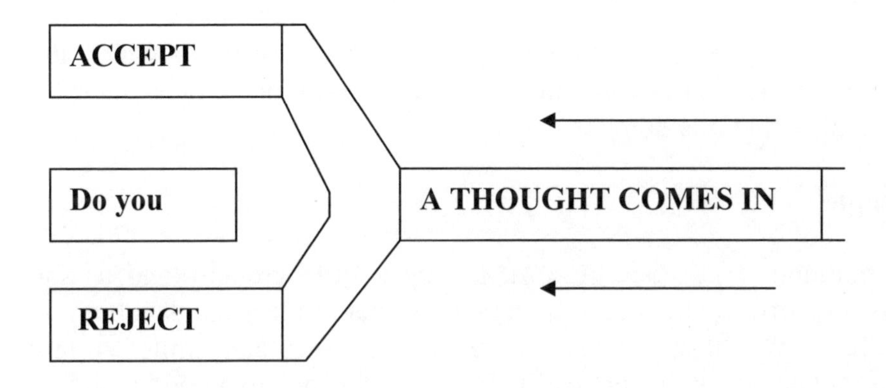

This example shows, in very simple terms, how a thought comes into your mind and the two choices you have to make when faced with whatever thought it is. For the purpose of this book, let's assume that the thought is something negative like "I am really fat and I hate myself". At this point you have hit the crossroads. What do you want to do; which way do you want to go? It's your choice: you can accept the thought, take it seriously and run with it, taking all of the negative consequences like feeling awful and dejected, analysing your body and then finding fault with it. Looking at the parts you don't like, comparing yourself to the so called "ideals" of the world like some of the waif super models who literally starve themselves with unhealthy diets that rob them of energy so that they have to take cocaine in order to be able get up in the morning.

Begin to question the ideals that you may have set in your mind; they might not be worthy of such attention.

Or do you reject the thought, understanding that this is just a silly thought that needs to be dismissed into the mental garbage can along with all the other worthless rubbish that pops into your mind? Maybe you are overweight and you do need to lose weight, but if you know that then you use the subconscious wisdom to guide you to the right solution rather than listening to the critical analytical chattering of the conscious mind. Your inner wisdom will guide you towards a sensible plan of action to help you improve your body, rather than the melodramatic " I hate myself", which the conscious mind tells you to think.

I'm going to give you a couple of examples of ways in which the conscious mind chatter can "monkey around" with our minds when we don't realise that it is doing it.

Example

One morning, Jane goes to work feeling a little grouchy and as she enters the office she hears a couple of her colleagues laughing at something. When she enters the room, they stop and smile. A few moments later she sees her boss and she doesn't look in a good mood. A simple thought pops into Jane's awareness, saying "People don't like me at work". This thought is now analysed. She rethinks and rethinks the thought in order to make some sense of it. Suddenly her conscious mind has found some references to back it up: the people laughing as she came into work and she thinks "Maybe they were laughing at me". Then this thought is analysed and the question "Why?" comes into play. And the mental analysis ball starts to roll; more and more, round and round, until Jane has found enough information to start to create a **belief** that people don't like her at work. Then, with this belief installed, she now views work as a threat and the people at work as conniving backstabbers. Soon her working relationships begin to break down as her odd behaviour towards her co-workers starts to show. After a few days her co-workers start to avoid her because of her "cold attitude" and this also works to validate her newly formed belief. This story could go on for months or even years, finally resulting in a miserable working life for Jane, and probably ending in resignation or dismissal. The lesson from this story is that one little silly thought, if taken seriously, can grow into something bigger and more destructive. I've seen people affected to the point of paranoia due to examples like this; people feeling like they are being singled out in some way. Remember, if you look for evidence, you will probably find some!

But if Jane had realised that a thought is just a thought and that you do have a choice whether you want to run with it (**accept** it or **reject** it), then a more satisfactory result would have occurred.

Another example

Tim is on his way home from work after a stressful day and his mind is still mulling over some of the more difficult aspects of the day. He begins to think about his wife and then remembers that she was a little cold with him the night before (his perception). Suddenly the thought "She might be having an affair" pops into his mind! Then his heart starts to beat as he remembers seven years earlier when, while he was seeing somebody else, he had the unfortunate experience of being cheated on by his then girlfriend. He remembers her "acting funny" a lot before he found out that she had been unfaithful and he now tries to match it up with the actions of his wife the night before. "Maybe **she** might be having an affair", he thinks, and then he starts to run a pretend movie in his mind of him catching his wife in bed with somebody else. Over and over the movie is replayed, with different scenarios and outcomes, maybe even violent confrontations of events that have not even occurred, and even if they did occur they would never be as dramatic as the ones he is imagining! Big dramatic fights and over-the-top dialogue help to make the thoughts seem even more powerful and emotionally charged, so by this time Tim is really worked up and ready to burst. Soon he is at the door of his home and he is now wound up. His presence is filled with tension. He asks his wife probing questions, looking for evidence and clues to catch her out to validate his suspicions! Pretty soon, a row breaks out and things come to a head. This continues night after night and a few months later Tim's poor wife files for divorce. All because a silly thought was allowed to be taken seriously in the beginning. If Tim had been aware of the thought systems of his mind then he would have been able to **dismiss** that silly thought and relax his mind when he got home from his difficult day, knowing that once he had relaxed he would be thinking clearly again. You must learn how to "accept or reject" your negative thoughts.

But how do I reject them?

This is also very simple. First, I'm going to give you some examples of how I do it, then how some of my successful clients have told me how they do it.

My Way

When a thought pops into my mind, which I recognise is a negative thought, which is not from my wise inner mind but from the conscious mind chatter, I mentally **hear** the word **"whooooooosh",** and imagine the thought flying away at the speed of light. Maybe it will come back into my awareness again seconds later, so **"whooooooosh"** it goes again. I do this as many times as it takes for the thought to go completely from my awareness as it goes into the mental "abyss" in my subconscious mind. I find that if you use both sounds and pictures to associate the dismissing process the subconscious learns very quickly that the thought is no good and remembers that thought is to be included into the garbage pile. The reason that we use pictures is because the mind tends to learn quicker with pictures than just sounds. That's why you can always remember a face and not always a name of a person. So you must use some kind of dramatic representation for the dismissing process. Every time I do this very simple exercise I am conditioning my mind so that it becomes a stronger habit the more I practise it. When something is repeated enough at certain times it then becomes a habit, which is then carried out automatically by the subconscious mind. Every time we dismiss a certain thought it trains the subconscious mind that this thought is not an important one and files it away into the garbage can of your mind.

When you reject your silly conscious mind thoughts you open the doorway to your subconscious wisdom.

This is great news, so what you are doing in effect is training your subconscious mind to carry out this process for you so that you don't have to consciously use the process any more, or very rarely because your subconscious mind has taken over by default. You have now trained your mind! You can go about your day without having to pay any attention to the chatter that used to affect you. So now you are thinking clearly, maybe for the first time in years, now using your inner wisdom to guide you. This is the mindset or strategy of every successful and wise person who has ever lived or is still living today, so if you want to be successful and happy too, you must adopt the same philosophy.

Here are some examples of how some of my clients use the dismissing thoughts process:

A male client told me that whenever a negative thought came to mind he imagined "blowing it away" with a six-shooter. He would hear the sound of the gun-shot, and would find it amusing and fun to do so (and they say that change has to be hard!).

A lady client who played tennis told me that whenever silly thoughts popped into her mind she would imagine smashing them with a tennis stroke.

Another lady told me she would imagine just pushing the silly thoughts into the sun and watching them dissipate.

A gentleman of 86 said that whenever negative thoughts tried to bother him he would waft them away in the same way you would waft away a fly in the garden.

A thought has about as much substance as a cloud passing through the sky.

You see, there really isn't a right or wrong way to do it; if it works for you, well, it's fine no matter what. The main thing is that you start to practise dismissing your negative thoughts right away: today, right now! You must begin to gain control of your thought processes as, once you do, I guarantee that you will be delighted with the results. One of the main things that I noticed after a few weeks of using this method was that I started to feel a wonderful feeling of real peace. I found my confidence levels beginning to soar and my relationships with friends and the people I love started improving. No more conspiracy theories or nagging self-doubts; I really started to believe in myself in a way I had never experienced before. Projects were now starting to materialise, which in the past had felt over-ambitious or maybe out of my league. I was finding that I was working better and smarter and both the quality of my work and the productivity were increasing. I couldn't believe what a difference it made now I was running my own mind correctly. I was making faster and better decisions than ever before and I felt and still do feel that my wisdom is getting stronger. I felt relaxed and clear-headed in situations where others were falling apart. A real sense of power comes over you when you learn to silence the critics in your head! What I have found also is that you keep on getting smarter and wiser as time goes by.

Does this sound too good to be true? I bet it does but I say this to you: you have nothing to lose and everything to gain for doing this, as **this process does not require any more effort than you are already using**. In fact, you'll find it takes less effort, as listening and reacting to the negative chatter of your conscious mind is tiring, time-consuming and energy-sapping.

There is always something to fear or worry about in the conscious mind, as it holds no wisdom.

Does this mean then that you walk around all day with a smile on your face, no matter what, like some type of moron?

Of course not! It doesn't mean that if somebody you love dies you just smile and pretend that it doesn't matter. Or if your marriage is going down the pan you just deny that there is a problem. Not at all. This new process helps you to see new solutions to problems by using the inner wisdom of your subconscious mind rather than listening to the manic chatter of the conscious mind. If my car is stolen I don't just smile and say "Oh that's O.K., I don't mind". I'll probably get mad for a few seconds then my wisdom will provide me with the appropriate action necessary to solve the problem. Would getting irate and shouting like Basil Fawlty, kicking my garage door and breaking my toe help to bring my car back to me or would it just leave me feeling stupid?

Only today I took my family out for Sunday lunch and when I got back I realised that I had lost my wallet with my cash and bank cards in it. I could have got really annoyed but I decided that I didn't want to spoil the day so after I looked for it and was sure it was lost I phoned the bank and cancelled the cards. It didn't turn into a drama and it didn't spoil what was a great day out. I just got on with it. You see, we can choose how we want to deal with a problem by simply deciding which way we want to go with it. If you don't want to fall apart or get annoyed, well, you don't have to. You just **choose** the way you **want** to react instead and then just do it. This is something that a lot of people have a hard time getting their heads around as they think that all of their reactions are automatic — maybe even genetic — as if the way we act is pre-programmed inside of us and there is nothing we can do to change our behaviour. "I can't stop myself; it's in my nature" is a typical statement used by the reactive person who hates taking responsibility for themselves. **They** blame everything — from their upbringing to the city they were born in and even their genes — for their behaviour. This wanting to shift responsibility from themselves, and to blame some other person or thing, is the norm for the reactive person. " She makes me hit her!" or "He didn't pick up his socks and that made me furious!" are some of the things I've heard in my time working with people. The proactive person, on the other hand, takes full responsibility for themselves so if they react badly for whatever reason they learn from it and decide that in the future, if a similar situation arises they will deal with it in a whole new, better way. Quite often the proactive person will mentally run through some alternatives in his or her mind until they arrive at a satisfactory alternative and then decide to do it next time. The proactive person knows that a new, better behaviour is just a new, better decision away. So, understanding the power of your choices plays a large part in changing your unwanted behaviours. We are constantly making choices without really being aware of it; we choose what to eat, we choose what to say, and we choose how to act.

Your thoughts change your energy levels

Have you ever noticed that whenever you have been in the middle of a negative thought cycle your energy disappears? Sometimes it feels like the life has been sucked out of your body and you feel exhausted. If you are or have been depressed, have you noticed that your energy disappears? If you're stressed out, your body feels fatigued but the adrenalin is keeping you awake, your body is aching for rest but your mind won't shut up. It is no real surprise to see how happy, positive-minded individuals seen to have boundless energy, where generally depressed individuals seem to be always tired and listless. This is because the very thoughts that we think have a direct effect on our body's energy fields. This simple fact cannot be underestimated in its power to influence how good we feel. Take a moment now to check your energy levels. How do you feel, energy wise, on a scale from one to ten, bearing in mind the time at which you are reading this book? If you are reading this in bed, remember how you felt at peak daytime today. Imagine the scale at ten brimming with energy and at one totally exhausted. Please do this, as this is important to the mind body connection. Whatever the number was, answer this important question:

What has your thinking been like over the past few days?

What was the theme of your thinking? Was it predominantly positive or predominantly negative? Really think about it, and see how it relates to your recent energy levels.

Chances are, if you have been feeling tired and listless recently, the theme of your thinking will have been negative, or if you have been feeling great and energetic your thoughts will have been predominantly positive. Think about this scenario. Imagine that you're very tired and you're lying on your sofa, trying to keep your eyes open as you watch the National Lottery draw. Your eyes lazily watch the numbers as they are put on the screen. Suddenly you think that you recognise these numbers and your eyes begin to widen! You sit bolt upright and your heart starts to beat, you're alert now and your energy has returned. You rush for your purse and hurriedly begin to search for the ticket. Yes, there it is! You run to the T.V. As you check the numbers, your heart sinks as you realise that, although similar, the numbers aren't the right ones. As you begin to curse in anger, all your old tiredness returns and you fall back on to your sofa and back into fatigue. How many times have you been feeling good and then you hear some bad news and then you feel drained instantly, or when you've been feeling down and then an old friend calls you unexpectedly and you perk up and feel great? How can this happen? Well, the obvious answer is that the thoughts that we think about when these things occur manifest into either energy or fatigue, depending on how you perceive the events.

People who live dull, boring thoughts have dull, boring energy levels: it's as simple as that.

Choose your thoughts carefully, as they control your life, your health and your happiness.

I've met so many unhappy and depressed people all through my different careers and the saddest cases of all are the people who think that the reason they are unhappy is due to the circumstances they are in and not their own thinking. To them, their depression is due to the world we live in and not their thinking and is due to the "reality" of it all. These people really have it the worst, and will almost definitely argue their case with clear-cut examples to validate their beliefs to help **you** see "the reality". To them, positive thinkers are not living in the real world and they will always want to be right in their arguments. They tend to moan most of the time about the injustice of this and that and constantly slag off people who are successful and happy. The need to be validated in their beliefs is paramount and they can always produce a hatful of stories to counter-attack any positive idea or thought you may put forward. If you know one of these people I will say this to you:

Do not waste your good, positive energy trying to change the viewpoint of the pessimist. You will only become frustrated.

Be at peace with the simple fact that these people probably will not change and that they are actually entitled to have their opinions just as you are to have yours. If **you are** one of those people yourself, I offer you this: you might not agree with me over this issue (which is your right) but ponder these truths:

1. **Positive thinking feels better than negative.**
2. **I know of no successful person on this planet who is a negative thinker.**
3. **Nobody wants to be around a negative, pessimistic thinker (only negative, pessimistic people).**
4. **Nobody wants you at his or her party.**
5. **You will probably die lonely.**
6. **You will look older than your years.**

7. **It takes no more energy to be positive than to be negative (actually it takes more energy to be negative; depression takes a lot of effort!).**

So you can take it or leave it: which way do you want to go? You can be depressed or happy — it's your choice.

When negative thoughts pop into your awareness you are then at a crossroads where a choice has to made.

We even choose the personalities that we have! If you are known as a hard man you choose to have the personality of a hard man. You walk that way, you talk that way and you give off the air of hardness: these are all choices. You may not be aware of doing it as you might have been doing it for so long that you can't remember starting it, but at some point you made a decision to be that way and chose to keep it. All the time I see people with quirky personality traits who seem to think they are convincing us that they are what they want us to believe. I know a woman who I grew up with in the same town as me who changed her voice and accent to that of a well-to-do socialite. She must have decided to change herself one day and she has now reinvented herself as a different person; the only problem with doing that is that people now view her as some kind of "fruitcake". This is down to a lack of self-confidence and can be remedied by following the principles outlined in this book.

It is vital that we endeavour to improve ourselves but this should not be at the expense of losing our identity.

We all know somebody like this, a person who tries to convince us (and themselves) that they are not who we think they are. The saddest part of this charade is that to other people it is so transparent and false. The solution to this is not to give up trying to better yourself but to learn to be yourself and be happy with who you are, **not living a lie**. This can be done in two ways: you can join a self-love class and go for meetings once a week for a couple of years, looking in the mirror and telling yourself positive affirmations every day, but not really believing them **or** you could **decide**:

"FROM NOW ON, TODAY, I'VE DECIDED THAT I'M GOING TO STOP CRITICISING MYSELF AND BRINGING MYSELF DOWN. IF I NEED TO CHANGE SOMETHING ABOUT MYSELF I WILL DO IT IN A CONSTRUCTIVE AND NATURAL WAY. I AM GOING TO BE THE TRUE ME AND NOT SOMEBODY WHO I TRY TO BE."

How many times do we try to act in accordance with what we believe other people expect us to be? When you try to pretend that you're something you're not, what you are communicating to yourself is that you're not O.K. as you are. Just be yourself and people will respect you more.

O.K., we've established that our THOUGHTS control our FEELINGS, but is that true in every case?

There is one exception to this rule, which is the **mood factor**. It is a fact of life, whether you are the most happy, positive individual on the planet or not, that you can't avoid the **mood factor**. For some reason, some days we wake up feeling down; this happens even if the day before you felt totally happy and at ease. Experts believe that moods are caused by chemical fluctuations in the body, which build up as time goes by due to various reasons. One reason is diet; when our bodies consume food this can affect us chemically as our bodies begin to digest whatever we put into our systems. The quality of the food we eat could be a contributing factor to this chemical process, so if we eat better-quality food this could help to lessen the probability of our moods. When I was younger I used to drink quite heavily on a Saturday night. The next day, when I was hung over, I would usually feel quite depressed and emotional. This mood would last until my body had got itself back to normal chemically. These days I hardly drink any more and I find that my moods are far less frequent.

Some days we wake up and feel low; it is a chemical biological phenomenon. Accept this as a part of being alive and the low feeling will lift more quickly.

Our bodies are like a ball of different chemicals, hormones and food, and balancing all of that is a complex business, but our bodies do a fantastic job (as long as we don't abuse them). Every now and then I believe the body gets out of synch and we are hit by a mood. These moods can be quite powerful and sometimes instant which tells us that they are chemical based and not thought-based. Thought-based moods take a little longer to develop and are usually not as emotionally charged. The chemical moods have nothing to do with the direction in which your life is heading or the circumstances in it. The moods which are chemical based, can hit you like a sledgehammer and will usually leave you asking yourself "Why do I feel this way?".

Asking yourself this question is a BIG mistake!

Asking yourself "Why?" whenever you hit a mood is a guaranteed recipe for disaster. Every answer that springs into your mind after asking that question will be negative. The worst thing you can do when you hit a low mood is to analyse "why" you feel like you do. **You will only come up with a negative answer.**

If you go looking for a reason for your mood you will probably come up with plenty of answers: your work, your partner, your kids, your friends, your parents, your home and your life in general will seem to be likely causes. The danger is to analyse any of these "likely causes" because if you do you will probably begin to find evidence in which to blame the mood! The day before the mood hit, these aspects of your life were fine but now, in this mood phase, they seem very annoying and overwhelming. Analysis is definitely a no-go area when you hit a mood as this will only drag it out and make it last longer. But there is a solution.

All the positive thinking in the world won't change a chemically based mood, so don't even bother trying. The way to survive a mood like this is to:

ACCEPT THAT YOU HAVE HIT A MOOD CAUSED BY A CHEMICAL FLUCTUATION IN YOUR BODY AND NOT BY THE EVENTS IN YOUR LIFE.

Even dogs wake up in a mood sometimes and they haven't read the newspapers or watched the news on T.V. to bring it on, so accept that it is a natural and unavoidable part of life. We might not like it but we have to accept that moods are just a part of being a human being. Accepting this fact is the first step to surviving our moods because, when we don't analyse them, it reduces the time it takes for the mood to lift. Take the diagram below, which shows how two different mindsets get different results from their different ways of thinking.

Figure 1: Using analysis

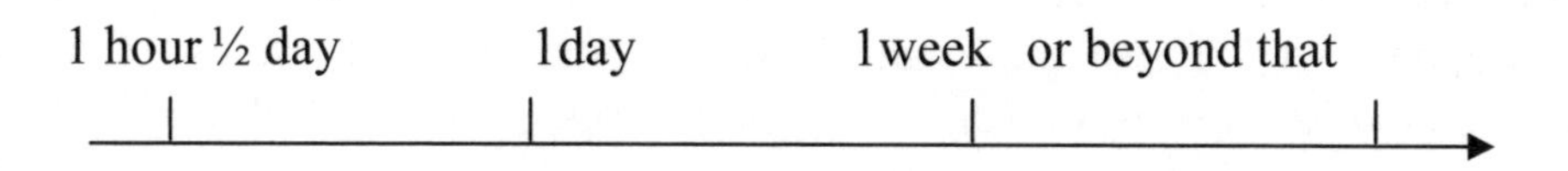

Figure 2: Accepting the mood as a natural chemical fluctuation

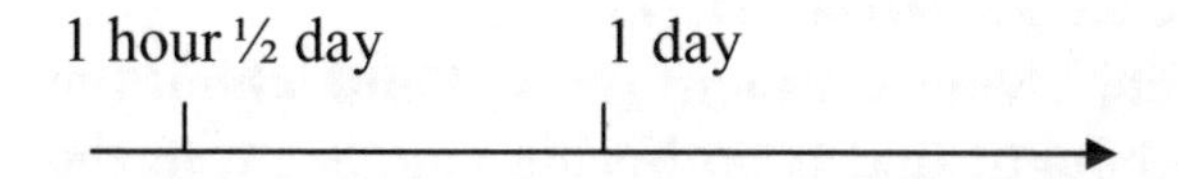

Understanding and accepting the simple fact that chemically induced moods are a way of life and that they occur in the most positive of minds will help to reduce the time span of a mood that **in the past** grew the more we analysed it. We can take a mood that may have lasted a week or beyond before, and reduce it to a day or even less just by accepting it and not trying to change it!

Special note!

It is not wise to make life-changing decisions when in the middle of such a mood, as decisions will usually be rash and **will not** be using the wisdom of your subconscious mind. The time to make these decisions is when you are back to your usual mental state, feeling clear-headed and using the eye-closing technique outlined earlier.

Eliminating stress!

The number one complaint that I hear in my office is that people are under stress. When the mind has too much on its plate we become stressed. The way we think about our lives and the challenges that we encounter along the way determine the way that we feel. When we try to think about all the things that we have to do at once, we become stressed. There is a better way to think about those things, though, without having the negative feelings attached. If you could think about whatever is on your mind without feeling stressed, then you will actually be able to do whatever you need to do without getting stressed about it. Sometimes we have thoughts that just seem that they do not want to go away, don't we? These annoying thoughts pop into our minds often when people annoy us or something bad happens to us. Below is an exercise that will help you to deal with stress and help to dampen down those annoying thoughts.

Stress Eliminator

1. **Find a quiet place, close your eyes and relax. Think about the stress or annoying thought that is bothering you. See it in the normal way that you have been thinking of it. Notice how you feel.**
2. **Imagine putting a frame of some sort around the stress or annoying thought so that it looks like a picture or a movie.**
3. **Mentally move it away in your mind's eye so that it is smaller and less "in your face". Notice how you feel. For most people this lessens the intensity of the feelings associated with the thought. Move it away further still, until you can look at it without any anxiety.**
4. **If there are still feelings of anxiety associated with the thought, dull the colour a bit and turn down any volume. Looking at the scene in your mind now, ask yourself this question: "What can I learn from this?".**
5. **When you have extracted the learning from the thought, mentally push it away so that it is tiny. Imagine pushing it into a black hole or something similar. Repeat the process of pushing the thought away whenever it pops up again, as this teaches the subconscious mind that this issue is now finished.**

Use this technique whenever troubling thoughts pop into your mind. It is very similar to the technique detailed earlier in this chapter and, once practised, can be used very quickly when you start to feel overloaded. When we take a big deal and make it a little deal then we are looking at it in its true perspective. We often blow things out of proportion in our minds so that to think about them gives us a headache. It's only when the anxiety has passed that we can realise that the thing that was the cause of our stress was not the thing that was bothering us at all but rather the way in which we were thinking about it. If everybody in the world was feeling stressed about it then the thing itself would be indeed a stressful thing but if it is just us or a few people affected then this it is us who are causing ourselves to feel anxious and not the event itself. It is always our **perception** that makes us feel stressed and not the event itself unless it is a universal reality.

Don't rely on unreliable people

How many times do we put our faith in people who always let us down? We rest our hopes on the dream that these people will come through for us, even though they have repeatedly let us down in the past. We live in hope that one day they will change and suddenly become reliable, even though historically they never have been. It is better, though, and more peaceful actually to know that it's our own expectation that needs to change and not those people. We must stop wanting them to change and accept them for what they are: unreliable. Once we label them in this way we will never have to face the feelings of disappointment again when they don't do something for us. Because we now expect it of them, we make other plans that don't rely on them coming through for us.

I have a friend called Marty. Marty is a great guy but the most reliable thing about him is that he will always let you down! For years this was a constant annoyance for me as he would always be late or forget to do something I asked him to do. One day, though, I actually relaxed and accepted that he would probably never change so I decided never to rely on him again. We are still as good friends but now I no longer become disappointed when he is late or whatever because now I make other provisions so that it doesn't affect me if he is. If we arrange to go out for a drink, rather than have to wait for a hour at the bar by myself I will arrange for another friend to be there too so if Marty turns up, that's great, but if he doesn't, it's no big deal.

This works out a lot better than hoping that people will miraculously change even though they never have. I urge you to use the same philosophy for the unreliable friends that you have, to make your life a lot less frustrated. Be at peace with the fact that people are unreliable and begin to rely on yourself more.

O.K., now that you have read this chapter it is important that you begin to start using the thought dismissing techniques outlined earlier. Do not go any further until you know and understand what to do. If necessary, read this chapter through again.

ChapterThree

Principle 3: Your Beliefs Make Your World

There is nothing more powerful in the human psyche than the power of our beliefs. They are the driving force behind everything that we do. What we believe is not universally true; it is true **only to ourselves** (what we believe). Beliefs can be the difference between us living successful fantastic lives or dull, mediocre ones without any real fulfilment. What we believe about ourselves is the most personal influential power we have, whether that is good or bad.

Who we believe ourselves to be, what we believe we can or can't do, what we believe our limits are or not and how we see ourselves as a total functioning person will determine the outcomes that we have in our lives.

To sum up the above paragraph: you become what you believe to be true about yourself. If you believe that you can't do something then that will become a reality in your life. If you believe that you have limits, whether they be physical or mental, that will become a reality in your life. These negative beliefs about yourself become the stumbling blocks that impede any future progress. You must begin to understand their power as it has an important role in creating a better quality of life for yourself. If you believe that the world is a bad place then this is what will be reflected back to you: such is the power of our beliefs. You will only be able to see the bad things that happen and will filter out any of the good, as you are not looking for the good, only for the bad. What we look for we find and when you believe that the world is a bad place you will find references to back up that belief. There are many good things happening around the world at any given moment but if you believe it is a bad place then you are not looking for the good thing so they go unnoticed. The person with this belief seeks verification of this belief and usually finds it.

"You are always a valuable, worthwhile human being, not because anybody says so, not because you're successful, not because you make a lot of money but because you decide to believe it and for no other reason."
Dr Wayne Dyer

Beliefs are the "daddies" of all psychological success and failure; they are the difference between first and second place in the race. What you believe your strengths or weaknesses are will reflect externally in the way you act. There is **nothing** more influential than what you believe. Your beliefs govern your actions so you really need to understand them and know how to change them if a belief that you have is affecting the quality of your life. Most people I speak to do not realise that they have these beliefs set up in the first place, which they use in everyday conversation to convey the way they see the world. A simple statement like "You can't teach an old dog new tricks" seems like a fairly harmless phrase but when we understand the power of beliefs we find that this is not the case. If we were to accept this common statement and believe it to be true, what would happen to us, as we got older? Would we begin to shy away from doing anything new or different because we now believe we can't do it, as we get older? And at what age do we decide this begins to take place: 40, 50, 60+? When? Well that depends on us, what we believe it to be.

A lot of false beliefs are passed down to us from many different sources: our parents and grandparents, neighbours and friends, and last but not least the good old media. Not all of them are malicious, but quite often almost unconsciously so, as in the same way that they were passed down to those people in the first place. What we have to be aware of is that we are constantly being programmed by opinions of various sources, such as the media, which, if we don't recognise this, we could become very negative in our thinking. Have you noticed that whenever you watch the news, the negative stories outweigh the positive stories by about 95 per cent negative to 5 per cent positive? Who selects which news they decide to report on? Surveys show that bad news is better for business than good news, so because all the media companies are looking for more profit they always lean heavily on the side of negativity. You could say that negative stories give them positive results! The more dramatically negative the news stories are, the more we want to watch them to see if they will have any effect or bearing on ourselves. If you were to believe all the news stories and nothing else you would believe that we were living in a world of murderers, rapists, crooked people and God knows what else. What the news people failed to report on was all the millions of positive things that happen around the world every single day and that are never reported because they don't "grip the viewers" and therefore bring in the money like the negative stuff does. The media always like to report some kind of impending disaster on the horizon. I remember when I as a kid it was reported that the world could be returning to and ice age. Now they are saying it's getting to hot! Make your mind up what's it going to be media please? Is an asteroid really hurtling to earth or will a giant underwater volcano really erupt and wipe out the Earth? This type of scaremongery has been in circulation since time began and we are still here! Every year a new one is invented and is pitched towards the ever cautious conscious mind thinker. Beware of it.

What we believe is the most powerful force we have; it's what we use to create our worlds.

Now, I'm not suggesting that the world doesn't have problems that are important and shouldn't be in the news — not at all. What I am saying is that it should be balanced fifty-fifty. That way we can work together to solve the problems we do have. That way we aren't overwhelmed by the task because of the constant negative bombardment of the media. Whenever we are overloaded with the negatives all of the time it seems impossible to solve any of them, so we give up. Protect yourself and protect your mind from the negativity of the media and don't let the news companies control your mind.

Think for yourself. This also goes for general television programmes too. Some programmes are made for the ever-cautious conscious mind thinker who watches those "real-life T.V." programmes with bated breath. Those "watch out for X danger" shows are peddled to the super-cautious conscious mind thinkers who then take this information and then install it into a belief. This drivel is shown with a view to help us but all it does is further reinforce the conscious mind's resolve to help us see the dangers of things that, in all likeliness, will never happen.

The amazing thing about beliefs is that we make them up! We take the evidence given to us from the experiences we have in our daily lives and formulate them into our belief system. For us to believe something we have to have some sort of evidence to back it up. If you believe you are unlucky, for instance, to make a statement like that you have to have some evidence or references in your mind to back it up. You cannot have a belief without some form of evidence to back it up: **"Well, remember this and that etc. …"**, as you start to recall events from your past, which to you will serve as proof to validate the belief, with every negative situation in the future serving and supporting the belief more and more, like another layer on top making it more solid. Once you have a belief installed you will find examples to back it up. But you failed to recognise the times when you were maybe lucky in your life, when things were going well, as you never paid attention to those times! That is the power of beliefs: they make you blinkered to any other possibility.

There is no greater influence in life than our beliefs. We see what we believe.

Lets take the example of being unlucky. If you really believe that you are, you may find yourself passing up opportunities that may have actually yielded fantastic results, but the thought "I'm always unlucky" pops into your mind and puts you off. The way of the successful person is to know first that there are no negative situations, only opportunities to grow and learn from. Secondly, luck is a "myth" which can rarely be repeated otherwise it is not luck at all but a skill. I urge you not to buy into the belief of luck but rather to put your faith in yourself; this helps you to gain self-confidence. Blaming luck is just another way of being reactive and shifting responsibility from yourself. I once spoke to a young man who told me that the reason he couldn't hold down a job was because of the "stars". He believed that his destiny was already mapped out by an astrology book he had bought two years earlier which told him he would have problems when working. Because he **believed** in the book, this became a self-fulfilling prophecy where he wouldn't turn up for work! I swear to you, this story is true! When I told him I was a proactive person and explained to him that it meant I took full responsibility for my life he looked horrified.

Recently I was speaking to somebody and mentioned that I was writing this book. At the end of the conversation this person said "good luck". I told him "Thanks, but I don't believe in luck. The success or failure of this book will not be down to luck but rather how well I write it and market it and for those I take full responsibility".

If you believe in luck you will soon begin to believe that you are unlucky.

What we believe we are capable of doing is the major driving force between success and failure. Do you believe that you are limited or do you believe that you can be whatever you want to be? The negative thinker would say it is better to be realistic about your limitations, saying that you have to know what they are (as if this is actually helping you to avoid some disastrous consequence by focusing on you limits). Proactive thinkers believe on the other hand that the only limits we have are the ones we **think** we have. The proactive thinker believes we have no limits, only new avenues to explore and new challenges to conquer. The proactive person never gives up even if it takes over 10,000 attempts like it took Edison to invent the lightbulb. What your beliefs are and what you believe in **will determine** the experiences that you will have in your life. What I am going to do now is give you some examples of different beliefs that people come to see me with all the time and explain what typically happens when you believe these beliefs.

Belief 1: I'm unattractive and unlovable

For females: This is a real humdinger of a belief and one that leads to much misery. The person who believes this typically dresses to reflect the belief, usually picking dull, frumpy clothes and wearing an old-fashioned hairstyle. They are suspicious of people who show interest in them and usually dismiss compliments. They don't tend to exercise and don't usually look after them selves physically, maybe becoming overweight which again helps to reinforce the negative belief that they are unattractive. If they are married they often live a daily battle of the husband trying to reassure the wife that she looks O.K. and her dismissing his comments as rubbish. Over time this becomes tiresome for the husband and he gives up, sex is a rarity and is viewed as a chore. All this adds up to a dull life.

For males: for the male who has this belief, he usually looks and dresses to reflect the belief also. He is usually introverted and does not make any real effort with his physical appearance, whether that be with his physical condition or the clothes he wears. There is sometimes a "feeling sorry for themselves" deep-rooted thought pattern at the bottom of it all, which prevents any movement into a more positive self-image mindset. This person avoids situations where a mate could be found because of their belief that nobody could find them attractive anyway, so why embarrass themselves trying? Sometimes the person with this belief is not introverted but actually an over-the-top extrovert. This personality type sabotages any chance of having a meaningful relationship by behaving in stupid ways, even anti-social ways like drinking to excess and acting stupidly. He acts as if his behaviour is out of his control and often says that "No woman can love me". Or he doesn't even try because he "knows" any attempt to find a mate will result in ridicule, so avoidance is the key. Often being lonely, he looks to escape this by creating hobbies or even unhealthy habits. Either way, again exercise isn't usually partaken or physical appearance is not favourable for attracting a mate.

Both sexes with this faulty belief system can be prone to acting like a "drama queen" sometimes, and are probably thought of as a pain in the butt by their long-suffering partners. What they don't realise is that their attitude and behaviour are a burden on every body else as they suffer along with it.

Belief 2: I'm not very smart

This is anther **great** belief as the person who believes it never progresses very far in life. This person shies away from anything that is mentally challenging for fear of failure and is usually employed in very low-paid jobs. This person definitely doesn't have the "learn from mistakes" mentality, and replays past unsuccessful attempts in an endless loop which helps to solidify the faulty belief. This person may have developed this faulty belief through early childhood parental programming or may even have adapted this for themselves as time went on. This person has an arsenal of readily available mental references to back up his or her belief and will reinforce it though the same negative thought patterns in their minds. This person may shy away from being the centre of attention and can be introverted, fearing they may be found out if they speak up. Or in the completely other end of the spectrum the person may be the joker or the lovable rogue, acting the fool and playing up to the part of the idiot. This person typically acts out the belief to the full, making bad decisions on purpose, not wanting to disappoint the people who expect it of them. Sometimes this person will be easily misled and may partake in criminal activities because of being persuaded easily. The person with this faulty belief installed rarely achieves past the point of average. If any of the above rings a bell with you, you may want to ask yourself if you want to keep having this belief.

Belief 3: If only I was rich then I could be happy

If this belief were true then every person who was wealthy would be tremendously happy and the more money they had, the happier they would be. I think we all know that this is not the case I reality. If it were true you wouldn't read about all the pop stars who regularly have to check into those expensive rehab clinics that cater for the rich. We regularly read about celebrities who receive the awards and money but then nearly die from a drug overdose. You read about lottery winners who get depressed because they cannot fit in with the new environments they find them selves in, often losing their old friends and then trying to fit in with the "Joneses" without much luck. Feeling lonely and out of place, they try to buy their happiness and usually find themselves broke in less than five years. So the truth is that money doesn't automatically buy your happiness; your happiness is determined by your **thinking**.

I'm not saying that having money isn't nice; we live in a Western environment where we need to earn a decent living in order to live comfortably. What I am saying, though, is that if you think that getting a new three-piece suite is going to make you happy or having the new car you saw gleaming in the showroom this morning is going to do it, you are wrong. These external things will only do it for a while and then the excitement will die and you have to look for the next (external) thing to keep you bolstered up! I never fail to be amazed at how many wealthy depressed people I see on a weekly basis. Others spend a lifetime wishing and wanting what they don't have, sometimes getting into debt to try to pretend they have money, and then resenting people who have what they want. Now if you can be wealthy and crack the mind thing, well then you will have a tremendous life, but don't make it an absolute must in the goal of happiness. If you do, you will be disappointed. So this is yet another faulty belief that people buy into. I urge you to dispel this belief if a life of inner peace and contentment is what you desire.

Belief 4: If other people would change then I could be happy

Yeah, right! The person who believes this one is a person who lives a life of constant disappointment. This person believes that the way **they** see the world is the correct way and that people who don't share the same views or beliefs as them are out of touch and need to be corrected. This person lives a daily battle of angry frustration with the futile need to correct the wrongs of the world and its people. The people who suffer this belief are generally bossy and thought of as a pain in the butt. They are usually moaners, even if they say that they are "very positive minded". They usually nag their partners, often putting them down, because they don't think like they do, hoping that one day they will change them. The idea that because we are all different therefore have our own perception on how we see life is generally recognised by such persons but never really fully understood or acted upon. This person will often argue their case aggressively to "prove I am right", with all of their predetermined references to back up their case all ready and waiting to be unleashed. They never really listen to the other person's point of view, but rather are preparing to speak when a gap comes into the conversation. This is due to the fear that the other person might say something of truth that may actually change their opinion. God forbid!

If you can relate to any of the above beliefs you must read the next paragraphs thoroughly and follow the belief change exercise. Even if you don't relate to the above, think of a negative belief that you don't like anyway and go through the exercise. You owe it to your self to do it.

Our beliefs are formed through the experiences and influences in our lives, good or bad. They are not based on a universal reality.

With all of the above negative beliefs and countless others, the person hanging on to them will be limited by them in some way or another. There are many different beliefs that people hold on to (often not knowing that they are) which can have a devastating effect on the quality of our lives. You must find what negative beliefs you have and get rid of them. "What, just like that?" did I hear you say? **Yes!**

There is also a belief that to change old, unwanted beliefs takes a long time, with years of painful therapy week after week, going through your past, looking for its origins. This is simply not true as changing beliefs is really quite simple; in fact just today I changed another one! All you have to do is have a small amount of evidence to make the new belief stick. Here's the simple process.

1. **Identify the old negative belief that you don't want any more.**

2. **Decide what new belief you would rather have instead.**

3. **Get some form of evidence in your mind to support the new belief or, if you can't, just imagine yourself in the future, acting out the new belief.**

4. **DECIDE that you no longer need the old belief and let it go with some sort of visualisation imagery.**

5. **Imagine that you now have the new belief installed and enjoy the feeling of having it, feel what it feels like then DECIDE to keep it.**

So that you understand just how to use this five- step formula, I'm going to run it through with you with a real-life negative belief. O.K., let's say you had an old negative belief that you can't control your finances. If you hold on to that one you will reflect that belief and be clumsy with your money. This is a very common belief that I myself used to believe was true about myself. The day I decided to stop believing that I couldn't handle my money very well and that I could never be a good money manager was a turning point in my life. I found my ability to manage my finances started to improve overnight. I started to look for references to back up my new belief and I was shocked to see how many I had! You can do the same. Please read through the five-step example on the next page to show you how to change dumb beliefs and then apply it to your own!

Step 1. You don't really want to be clumsy with your money so you make a decision that you no longer want or need this belief.
Step 2. Decide what you would like to believe instead, bearing in mind that you make up all of your beliefs anyway and what ever you believe doesn't make it universally true. Let's say we make the new belief something quite reasonable like " I am a good money manager", even if you don't believe it this is what you want instead, so you decide to keep it.
Step 3. Think of some time in the past when you did manage some money well and reflect on that, no matter how small and trivial the episode was. Think of yourself as being a good money manager and imagine the future with this belief and how it will affect you (positively).
Step 4. Think about the consequences of keeping the old negative belief versus the new constructive one. Decide to get rid of the old belief and use some kind of imagery to let it go. Maybe imagine writing the old belief down on paper and then throwing it into an open fire, hearing it hiss and scream as you exorcise the demon. Gone forever!
Step 5. Now open your mind to the possibility of having the new belief "I am a good money manager", and imagine that you now are and see yourself performing with this new belief in the ways you would be performing if you had it. Make the decision to accept it, even if you don't 100 per cent believe it yet, as, once you do it, the evidence will come by itself by virtue of your having the belief!

Please note: The sceptic might say that this is self-delusion or denying the truth. This is not the case at all; one belief will keep you immobilised and stuck in the past and the other (new) one will move you towards the belief itself, which will definitely become a reality as you now become responsible for that belief. I have changed so many beliefs quickly and effortlessly in this way, and **even more easily than that**. You will too as you get used to this very simple process. I have also taught this to literally hundreds of clients who have had mental blocks that had prevented them from excelling to the extent I knew they were really capable of. I have helped people such as athletes, government speakers, teachers and business men and women who wanted to climb the ladder. With all the above examples it was their **old beliefs** that stopped the way to progress.

You can only change your beliefs if you want to

One of the hardest things to do is to change the belief system of somebody who doesn't want to change it. When clients come to see me with their various challenges, more often than not there are certain beliefs which must be changed before any other work can be done. In the clinical setting this is usually done quite easily as the person must expect or want to change something otherwise they wouldn't come to see me. But what if you have some beliefs that you don't want to change? If, for instance, you had your heart broken in a relationship, you may now believe that all relationships will be the same and so then you avoid them all together. This belief then serves as a protection device, with your references to back it up. Another challenge is when you try to change a faulty belief in somebody else. When you challenge them what you are actually saying to them is that everything they have come to believe that was true their whole life was wrong, and not many people will just accept that! Now with some people this would be a time for great joy; a chance to start a fresh with a new perspective but for others who have had these beliefs this is a time to become very defensive and aggressive. Religion must be the most powerful form of belief there is, where a person who believes a certain religious criterion will not budge from their standpoint. No matter what counter-argument is put forward, the person with the strong religious belief will not yield one bit. The idea that what they have studied and invested all of their time in is wrong would outrage that person. In the past this has been why countless wars have started. People will always defend their beliefs, especially if they have had them all their lives, because to admit that they were wrong would perhaps make them feel foolish. This is why people always have some references to back up their beliefs in case of a counter-argument.

Changing our beliefs is just allowing another perceptional doorway to open. The more doors that open, the clearer the direction is.

Let me tell you my story. In my own life, when I was younger I came to the realisation that I too had lots of old negative beliefs inside me that were affecting the quality of my life. My self-confidence was badly affected by these old beliefs and it showed. The one that I really strongly believed was that I wasn't very clever. I knew that if I dragged this belief around with me for the rest of my life it was really going to impede my future. I had certain standards of living that I wanted for myself but I knew they could never be realised if I believed I wasn't clever. So one day I took all my negative beliefs that I didn't want any more and wrote them down on a piece of paper. There were about ten or so old beliefs, which were really negative and limiting, and I looked at them. In doing so, I thought about the cost of having them. I looked at the cost in the past, the cost in my present life and the cost in the future for me if I didn't get rid of those beliefs. Looking at them there on paper made me understand the power of our beliefs so I decided to take charge of my life and get rid of them once and for all. I took one last look at them and realised that they had not served me in any way so I was sure that getting rid of them could only be a wise decision. I began to tear up the piece of paper into tiny pieces and smiled as I did so, feeling an immediate sense of relief. Then I took another piece of paper and wrote down ten beliefs I would like to believe instead. These new beliefs were much better and the opposite of my old beliefs and also a lot more satisfying so I committed myself to installing these new beliefs instead. I have never since gone back to believing those old beliefs and I now can't even remember what they were!

Once I made the decision that I wasn't going to have those beliefs any more, they no longer figured in my life. It was as simple as that! And why not? Who makes up the rules anyway, and who determines how long it should take to destroy a negative belief that we have? If you are in therapy and through the course of that you discover that you have some negative beliefs about yourself that are limiting your life, what do you do? Once you've found them out, how long do you want to keep them before you decide to dump them? Some people like to go on for weeks and months, even years, before they finally give them up. My question is: if you have found them out and decided that you need to get rid of them, why wait? The only thing that could prevent us from doing that is the **belief** that "you can't do it that fast", which is not true. If you're going to do it at some point anyway, why not **do it now**?

You can do this too with your limiting beliefs. Let me show you how!

Ridding Yourself of Old Limiting Beliefs

1. **Take a piece of paper and write down all your limiting beliefs. Look at them and ask yourself "Do I want to keep these with me as a part of me forever?". The answer must be NO!**
2. **Think about what the consequences in the past have been from having these beliefs. Think about how your life has been affected by these beliefs and the misery that they have caused. What negative effects did they cause with regard to your personal life, professional life and your relationships?**
3. **Think about the effect on your life now from having these beliefs. How is it affecting your life now and who else are they affecting in your life? Think about this with great emotion and do it thoroughly.**
4. **Think about the effects on your future if you keep these beliefs. What will your life be like in the future if you live by these old beliefs? What kind of state will your life be in and what type of quality of life will you have? Really think hard about this and imagine the years ahead with these old beliefs still dominating your life.**
5. **Ask yourself if you want to keep these beliefs and still have them figuring in your life or not. When you're sure that you don't want them any more, tear them up vigorously into tiny pieces of paper and feel good about it!**
6. **Now take another piece of paper and write down what you would like to believe instead. You can make these new beliefs as outrageous as you like, as you make up all of your beliefs anyway. Make them the opposite of your old beliefs.**
7. **Look at these new beliefs and feel good about adopting them. Even if you don't believe them right now, decide to believe them anyway and make them your daily focus. When you start to believe these new empowering beliefs they will start to become true. Now live your life as if these new beliefs were true. Read these new empowering beliefs through every morning when you wake up, to condition the new beliefs further.**

What really prevents us from doing something like this? Nothing. As soon as I decided that I didn't want my old negative beliefs any more, I took all those old beliefs and turned them around into the **opposite direction** so the belief that I wasn't clever turned into "I am intelligent" and so forth. It was a little strange at first but the more I began to accept and believe them, I found the new beliefs actually became true. I did become more confident and all the other things that I wrote down and began to apply just started to fall into place too. That doesn't mean that I didn't need to do anything to help towards their realisation — not at all. I continued to and still look for ways to improve myself further. Now I can honestly say that my ability to learn and understand new information has increased by at least 400 per cent, just by dumping my old limiting beliefs. I now believe in myself and don't put any mortal above myself in status or intelligence. Because of this new, healthier belief system I find myself doing much more varied activities and interests that in the past would have seemed daunting or "just not me". You can be the same.

Your beliefs influence the choices that you make; the more you believe in something the more you will see it.

One of the beliefs that I had when I was training to be a therapist was that I had a poor memory and I have since learned that a lot of people believe the same. I believed this so much that a month before starting college I called my tutor personally and pleaded with him to hypnotise me so that I could remember the upcoming information! He just laughed at me and told me to not be so silly. This is a common negative belief that I hear nearly every day both from both clients and from everyday people that I meet. The truth of the matter is that there is **nothing wrong with your memory**. It is just that you haven't concentrated fully on whatever was said or written. If your mind is on other things than what you want to remember then your mind thinks that that must be unimportant and places it in the "unimportant" section of your mind. Ponder this: how many things do you **remember** every day that you take for granted and never think to point this fact out to yourself? I bet that this morning you remembered to put your underwear on and brush your teeth, didn't you? How many times have you remembered the things that you had forgotten about? Can you recall that? Think about it: you pull yourself down for forgetting things, yet you remember much more and never give yourself a pat on the back for doing so. I have people come to see me all the time and list all of the things that they had forgotten to do! To that I usually say to them: "Please tell me about all the kinds of things that you **recall** forgetting about" or "Can you **remember** the last time you forgot something?". I do this to show them how good their memory really is. The fact is that we remember to do about 95 per cent of the things we need to do but we take it so for granted that we only remember about the things we forget. Confused? Think about it. Here are some tips that I have used that have helped me to sky rocket my memory retention power by over 400 per cent. Some of these simple concepts I learned on Kevin Trudeau's brilliant *Mega Memory* home study course; the other stuff I can't remember where they came from! Ha ha.

Tip No. 1: Begin to believe that you have super-powered memory. Even if you don't believe it, tell yourself that it is so and act and think as if it were true. If people ask you "How's your memory?" tell them that it's excellent and soon it will be true. This has to be tried to be believed!

Tip No. 2: Remember times when your memory was excellent and use them as your references for the new belief.

Tip No. 3: When you read something, imagine hearing the author reading it to you in some place you might imagine they may live or have lived, or imagine yourself reading it out in front of an audience. The point of this exercise is so that you are fully concentrated in what you are reading and not thinking about what you have to do later that evening! It stops the chatter.

Tip No. 4: Remember that the tense mind prevents the natural flow of information, so relax and don't try to force out the information you want. Relax and it will flow out. Have you ever come out of an exam to find that, now that you have relaxed, you can remember all the answers? This is because now that you are relaxed your mind is able to release the information which previously was locked in because of the build-up of tension. Relaxation is the key to memory retention and recall.

How to be dynamic!

Recently I was at the cinema with my wife and when the movie finished everybody stood up and most walked out of the wrong door. Everybody except my wife and I and maybe about five others walked out of the back exits and straight into the car park. The urge to follow the masses and go out of the wrong door was immense, but I could not allow myself to do it just because the majority were doing so. I remember later that night thinking about lemmings and how they follow each other as they jump off the cliff and I decided that as long as I believed in what I was doing in my life then I didn't care how far from the crowd it took me. When I first decided to become a therapist I had to suffer the usual negative comments from the doubting Thomases but, being dynamic, I didn't need anybody's approval as long as I believed it was the right path to take. I knew I would encounter some opposition along the way, as every other successful person the world over has, but as long as I believed in my dreams then I was prepared to ruffle a few feathers! If **you** want to be dynamic you must be prepared to do so this too.

When I have studied the character traits of the most successful and dynamic people of the world, the one thing that always stands out with **all** of them is that they have very different beliefs from those of the average person. These beliefs can be the driving force for changing things that they truly believe in, which to the average person sometimes seems impossible to change. To follow your beliefs when the rest of the world is trying to put you off is one of the biggest factors in the mental make-up of the dynamic person. The more people try to discourage them, the stronger their resolve goes; it's almost like other people's disbelief is the fuel for the fire as they blast through the walls of conventionality. A dynamic person usually has very different views from those of the average person, and quite often faces ridicule until they are proved right and then hailed as a genius. These people do not follow the crowd just because the majority do so. These people do not follow directions; they are direction changers and are constantly ahead of the game.

When we search for the truth regardless of whether or not it's the current thinking, we are truly on the right path to greater wisdom.

Whenever the impossible is proved to be possible — like breaking the four-minute mile, which at one time was thought of as not humanly achievable — it then becomes probable that others will do the same. Before the four-minute mile barrier was broken the belief that it was impossible to break was certainly the real barrier and not the physical feat itself. One man did not believe in the impossibility theory was Roger Bannister who broke the barrier on 6th May 1954. Once he broke it, many people broke it soon after. Dr Martin Luther King was another dynamic person who died trying to change the minds of the people of the world. He was a man of very strong beliefs and a very strong sense of his goals. His strength and conviction helped to change the world's view on racism. Racism in all its forms is another way in which beliefs can be destructive. The belief that a person from another country or culture is good or bad is what prevents us from uniting and loving each other without prejudice.

"Darkness cannot drive out darkness; only light can do that. Hate cannot drive out hate; only love can do that."
Martin Luther King

The dynamic Bill Gates of Microsoft had a very strong belief that he would be successful even though he left school with hardly any grades. What Bill was able to accomplish is a true testimony to the power of beliefs. If Bill Gates had had the belief that you could not be successful without a high academic background then that belief would have impeded his success and he would not be what he is today. Recently I watched a documentary about the life of Kevin Keegan who was a very successful English footballer who went on to be the national coach. One of the things that interested me about the documentary was that before Keegan could become a professional footballer there were three rather large hurdles for him to climb. The first hurdle was that he was very small in height; the second was that he wasn't very well built; and the final hurdle was that he wasn't very good at football! None of these things seemed to matter to him as his belief in himself and his dream of becoming a great footballer were greater than any limitation he appeared to have. He couldn't do much about his height but his body and his football skills were definitely things he could improve upon, which he did. With sheer unshakeable determination, Kevin built up his body to a fantastic level and he became one of the best footballers in the world in his time.

If we believe we have limitations these limitations will become our reality; if we believe that limitations are made for breaking this will be our reality also.

With all the dynamic people I have studied — whether they be great communicators, business people or athletes — the one thing in common they have is that they have the tenacity to overcome any obstacles that others may believe are too tough to climb. Oprah Winfrey is one of the most dynamic and successful women in America, and a woman I admire greatly. Oprah had a very difficult time as a child, coming from a poor background, at a time when your colour was a major limiting factor in finding a good job. Oprah turned around all of her so called "limitations", such as her weight, colour and background, and became the owner and presenter of her own daytime T.V. talk show which at the time of writing is still the most popular in America and is aired all over the world. She has starred in many movies, including ones produced by Steven Spielberg, and is said to have amassed a personal fortune of hundreds of millions of dollars! This woman is a testimony to the true power of belief and sheer determination.

The dynamic person not only wants to overcome challenges but lives to do so and actively seeks them out. This is the driving force that spurs them on. Without challenge the dynamic person is not living dynamically. Don't ever hope or want yourself to succeed; **know** you're going to do it! That's the difference. My motto to my clients is: "Don't hope it's going to work; **make it work**". When we believe in ourselves it is nothing to do with being big-headed or cocky; it is about finally allowing ourselves to be what we are all really capable of being. Do not fear believing in your true potential embrace and seek it out. It's waiting for you to collect; all you have to do is believe in yourself even if others don't! That is the characteristic of the **NO DOUBT** person.

The person who is truly dynamic acts without hesitation yet makes the right decisions. He or she does not act dynamically to impress others but lives this way as a matter of course, without knowing anything different.

The Five Characteristics of Dynamic People

1. An unshakeable resolve to do whatever they set out to do, regardless of whether or not it seems possible.
2. Unbreakable self-confidence in their own ability to do whatever they need to do.
3. Thinking positively and doing things differently to the average person.
4. Getting really excited by the prospect of fulfilling their goals rather than going down the pub or watching T.V.
5. Nothing can put them off; they view setbacks as merely stepping-stones on the road to success.

"Success is simply luck, ask any failure."
Earl Wilson

Chapter Four

Principle 4: You Get What You Focus On

As the title of this chapter says, you get what you focus on. This simple fact **cannot** be underestimated in its power to influence the results that we get in our lives. I know of no successful person in this world who isn't focused. To be successful though, you must focus on the right things.

"What you think about is what expands."
Dr Wayne Dyer

Ponder the above statement by the wise Wayne Dyer and think about what it means. What does it mean? What it means is that whatever you choose to focus on, it will grow with attention.

Problems

Let's take problems, for instance. The more you focus on the problem itself and not the solution, the more you will find that your problem will grow. This is a fact which I have seen demonstrated so many times when clients come to see me with their problems. I find that they have focused entirely on those problems which, as a result, got bigger. I would even go so far as to say that about half of my clients are there because of this negative focusing.

Think of a problem you have now or remember a problem that you used to have. Please put down this book and do this now!

O.K., if this problem is an ongoing one, ask your self this question: how long has this problem been my focus? Think about it; is the problem bigger now than it was before or is it smaller? If it's bigger then you are focused on it; if it's smaller then you have decided to try to forget it or you have solved it. One of the things I found to be true very early on was that people do not focus on solving their problem but instead they focus on the actual problem itself. This may seem like a natural thing to do but the very act of focusing so much attention on a problem is like pouring petrol on a fire. It gets **bigger**! Let's say, for example, that you have a problem communicating with people, and certain words are hard for you to say. Do you think it will help you to think about yourself struggling with those words in situations that you don't want to be in, replaying the thoughts over and over again every day? No, of course not, but this is what people do. The trouble is that most people aren't aware that they are doing it. Some people go into a daydream and, without knowing it, negatively start to program the unwanted behaviour to occur by the act of thinking and focusing on it. This almost unconscious thinking is detrimental to happy living so it must be recognised and stopped before it causes mental anguish.

When we focus on a problem with a view to solving it that is like trying to put a fire out by pouring petrol on it.

Thoughts are fast — lightning fast — and most people don't realise that these thoughts pop into their minds in the first place. The thoughts come and go but the feelings stay; this is because feelings last much longer than thoughts. These thoughts are nothing more than the conscious mind's chatter and should be dismissed in the way described in Chapter 2. They do not come from your wisdom; your wisdom would tell you the way to sort out your problems. Now, if you were an athlete and you were focusing on yourself winning a race then this would be **constructive focusing**, but if you're not and you're thinking about a problem that you have then this is **negative focusing**. So if, as Wayne Dyer says, what you think about is what expands, then all the negative stuff that you don't like is going to get bigger!

Let's take the example of Lucy. For years Lucy had been overweight and had focused a lot of her attention on trying to lose weight by lots of different means. She had been on so many diets over the years, losing lots of weight and then putting it back on (and a bit more) after the diets had finished. She'd tried high-carbohydrate diets, low-carbohydrate diets, starvation diets and detoxification diets — all had some success but, in time, the weight came back on when she returned to her regular, unhealthy eating patterns. That is because with all of these diets it was the restriction of food that had caused Lucy's weight loss and not the "miracle" diet itself. She was a very determined woman who would never give in and every day when she awoke she began the daily "weight war", which started with her standing on the scales. Then she would tell herself that she could conquer the cravings for food that she knew would be there during the day. This would go on throughout the day. All the while Lucy was feeling more and more low as the strain of it all began to take its toll. Then **boom**! A sudden urge, and then she began to eat. Chocolate after chocolate went into her mouth as she medicated her stress with the reward (chocolate). Suddenly the pressure was released and she felt relieved, but an hour later the guilt set in as she looked at herself in the mirror. She felt terrible and became upset about her the size, but she reasoned that tomorrow would be a new day, and then the battle could start all over again.

This is a hopeless and totally wrong way to try to sort out your problems. If Lucy wanted to live a great life with fun and happiness then those things were what she should be focusing on, but if Lucy focused on trying to control her weight and her eating habits then this is what "expanded". You must focus on the **SOLUTIONS**.

When we focus on our problems they get bigger; the more we do this the more they begin to take over our lives. The time to solve problems is when we relax and find a quiet place — then the subconscious wisdom is called upon. Trust its wisdom.

Remember that answers to problems cannot usually be found by using the conscious analytical mind. The answers are located in the subconscious wisdom. If Lucy had used her inner wisdom to guide her through her weight problems she might have been surprised by how simple the solutions to her weight problems were. Let's suppose that Lucy did use her inner wisdom, and after closing her eyes and relaxing she asked the question: "Subconscious wisdom, I require your help to help me lose weight. What do I need to do in order for me to do that?". Here are some of the simple answers that her mind may have told her:

- **You need to start to exercise regularly and join a keep fit class.**
- **You need to stay on good, fresh, healthy food.**
- **You need to practise mental relaxation when you feel stressed.**
- **You need to focus on something other than your weight (such as enjoying life!).**

There are lots of professional people, such as myself, who can help you to solve whatever you want to change in your life. These days we have more choice than ever. If you adopt these principles into your heart and use them you will never need to see people like me. One of the things that I do know, though, is that if you've had a problem for a long time you've now probably mentally conditioned it into your everyday thinking and it must be de-conditioned.

How do we do that?

It's time for a new focus in your life. Something dramatically different, something exiting or challenging and fun! Yes, you've had the same old 50,000 thoughts a day regurgitating around your thinking for too long and **now** it's time for some new stuff. Your life had become predictable and boring, living in "tunnel vision", doing the same old stuff and thinking the same old thoughts and now it's time to change the course of your life. Now, if your life is fulfilling and exiting, well then, you're already on the right track but if it isn't, now is the time when we need to make some changes. The problem is that when you're feeling down or stagnating you will always find excuses for not doing anything. The usual excuse I hear all the time is "But I don't have the time to do anything else". Think about this. If you have time to have your problem then you have time to do something to solve it! As everything else in this book explains, you have to **do something different** if you want something to change. As the old saying goes: **"If you do what you always done, you will get what you always gotten"**. So the message in this is that it's time to get off your butt, it's time to start taking some chances and start experimenting with life. It's time to see what's on offer, remembering that the only thing that could stop you from doing that is your **beliefs**, as we discussed in the last chapter. **So there's no excuse not to do it now!** Remember that we make our beliefs up, and we can believe what we like, so why not start to believe that we have the potential to do anything that we want to?

Whenever we think about doing something we have never done before we get funny feelings, don't we? These feeling are usually located around the stomach and when we get them we usually do one of two things:

1. **Avoid whatever it is like the plague.**
2. **Run towards it.**

Which way you go will be determined by how you represent the feeling you have. If you label the feeling "fear" you probably use Number 1. And if you label it "excitement" you will use Number 2 and run towards it. The funny thing is that often the two feelings are the same; the only thing that is different is that every person labels them both differently. One person has learned to call the feeling "fear" and the other person has learned to call it "excitement". The label you give the feeling will give you different results from your different interpretations. But — and it's a big but — what if you got the message wrong, what if the label you gave the feeling were wrong? What if you mistakenly gave it the label "fear" when the feeling was really excitement? What if you **did** get it wrong?

One person who helps to clarify the situation is the brilliant Anthony Robbins. In his *Lessons in Mastery* program, he talks about thinking about our feelings in a whole new way. One of the ways he talks about is to begin to understand that there are no negative feelings, only signals that our bodies are trying to tell us that we need to make a change. He says that these signals are telling us that we need to change either our **perception** or the **procedure** that we are using. He says that we can now call any feeling that we used to call negative an:

ACTION SIGNAL.

These are signals that tells us that we need to make a change, either in our perception (the way we are thinking), or our procedures (the way we do things). This is a very powerful way of thinking that helped me to change the way I viewed my old feelings. Using this way of thinking, I have actually been able to change the way I feel into more positive and resourceful ways when dealing with difficult situations. By changing my feelings into action signals I began to view them as my allies and not my enemies. I begun to understand the signals, which told me about the way I was thinking.

Your feelings are the signals that tell you how you've been thinking. They are the messages from your body.

To show you what I mean, I have used what Anthony says in his program and created a model from it so that you can use it too. This model has ten of the most common feelings that in the past would have been thought of as negative but now we can call action signals. Although there are obviously more feelings than the ten I have written down, these feelings seem to represent the **core** of most of our unwanted feelings. This model is a fast and easy way to change the way you feel and it gets easier and faster the more you use it. I have used this very simple technique quite extensively whenever I do something a little out of the ordinary, like public speaking. If I get a feeling that I don't like, I can change it very quickly by changing either my perception of what's going to happen at the event or the procedure that I was going to use. I find this technique is so simple that my feelings can change from uncomfortable to confident in a matter of seconds.

Use this model whenever you have feeling that you don't like. Maybe there is a party coming up about which you have some mixed emotions about or an interview in the pipeline for a job promotion about which you feel a little tense. Whenever you feel an emotion that you don't want to feel, you can change it in seconds by using this easy formula. Take some time and think of something that may be bothering you or something about which you have some strong emotions. If you want to change it then use this simple formula, and as you get used to it you should experience a new paradigm shift in the way you view your feelings. I have taught this new way and used this same model with many of my clients and the majority have said that it has helped them. It may take a little practice to remind yourself to do the technique, but the more you do it the more it then becomes just habit.

You will see there are three columns under the heading "**THE EMOTIONS**".

The first column is "Feeling", which describes the feeling that you have at the thought of something. This column shows the ten feelings that are at the **core** of all negative feelings that are typically felt by people when they say they feel bad. If the feeling you are experiencing isn't in the "Feeling" column, like "I feel stressed", you may find that the **core** feeling is that you feel frustrated, for example, which **is** listed in the column. Perhaps you might find that the core feeling of stress to you is anger, so identify the core feeling in the left-hand column.

The second column is the "Meaning". This column outlines in simple terms what the feelings mean when you get them. It is important for us to understand what these emotions mean so that we can proceed to the next stage.

The third stage I call the "Remedy" stage where we use a five-step procedure for change, starting with:

The Remedy

1. **Identify the signal. Find out which action signal you are sensing.**
2. **Appreciate the message. Understand that, whatever action signal you receive, there is a message in there, so be grateful for the communication.**
3. **Get curious about it. What does it mean?**
4. **Clarify what you want. Do I really want to feel this way?**
5. **Take action! There are really only two things that need to change and they are either:**

Your perception: the way you are seeing things. Are things really as bad as you are painting them? Are you blowing things out of all proportion? Do you need to cut yourself or other people some slack? Do you need to chill out? Do you need to change your perception of this event?

Your procedure: the way you are doing things, or perhaps not doing things, as the case may be. Do you need more information before you start something? Do you need to prepare more? Do you need to start practising some new behaviour? Do you need to try something different?

The answers to these questions will help to change the way you feel about your feelings. This process is a very positive procedure that gets to the root causes (perception or procedure) very quickly and helps you learn as you change.

When we come to understand ourselves we come to realise that messages are given to us all the time, sometimes mentally and sometimes physically. When we become more in tune with ourselves we can understand and appreciate the messages we receive.

Take a look at the formula on the next page and use it to change how you feel when you receive an action signal. When you do you will begin to view those feelings in a new light. No longer will you resent them but instead now you will respect them and appreciate the action signal.

“THESE FEELINGS ARE SIGNALS THAT TELL US THAT WE NEED TO MAKE A CHANGE”

Anthony Robbins

THE EMOTIONS

ACTION SIGNALS

Feeling	Meaning	Remedy
1.Uncomfortable feelings:	Any moderate to strong sensations of discomfort (worry, stress etc)	1.identify the signal
2. Fear:	Signal to prepare or deal with some negative consequence of something about to occur	2.Appreciate the message 3.Get curious about it
3. Hurt:	An expectation has not been met and you have a feeling of loss	4.Clarify what you want
4. Anger:	A rule has been violated by somebody or yourself and you feel angry	5.Take Action! By either:
5. Frustration:	A change is needed in your approach in order to achieve your goals	↓
6. Disappointment:	An expectation has not been met	CHANGE PERCEPTION
7. Guilt:	you have violated one of your own rules or standards	or CHANGE PROCEDURE
8. Inadequacy:	Is a feeling of **less than** or lacking in some area	
9. Overloaded:	You need to re-evaluate what is most important in your life	
10. Lonely:	You need a certain kind of connection with people	

Make your health your priority

Most people understand this principle and even agree with it but not enough people actually live their lives by it. I know of no dynamic, successful, happy person who doesn't have this principle at the top of his or her list of priorities. I wonder why? Is it just a coincidence that these super-successful people choose to look after their health when so many of the not-so-successful do not? I don't think so!

The answer is this. The successful person understands that to perform at the top level in every aspect of our lives we must have excellent health. We simply cannot perform at our best if the vessel that we carry around with us (our body) is not maintained and looked after. I see many people spend hours every week tuning and polishing their cars but spend little if no time looking after themselves. There is something wrong with the equation here. If your car's engine seizes up you can go out and buy a new one, but if your heart goes "pop" you are in serious trouble! It's not enough to be happy and content with yourself and abuse your body at the same time. If you want to reach your goals, what would be the point if you couldn't enjoy them with good health when you achieved them?

Without our health the whole plan goes to pot. You cannot buy it back when it's gone.

Whenever I speak of these matters to my clients, more often than not I see them begin to lose interest. It's a subject that people either love or hate but regardless of whether you like it, I'm going to write about it anyway. It's too important a subject just to dismiss. One of the things people tell me all the time when I ask if they exercise is that "I get enough exercise at work, I never stop I'm on my feet all day long". This may be so but unless your heart rate is elevated to a certain point **it is not the same as exercising**! As much as you may want to believe that it is, **it isn't**. It is **essential** to exercise regularly if you want to live the best life ever. Here's why:

1. It retards the ageing process.
2. It keeps your heart healthy.
3. It builds your self-confidence.
4. You gain more stamina.
5. You will look better in clothes.
6. You will look younger.
7. You gain more energy.
8. It's good for your bones.
9. You will live longer.
10. You will feel sexier.

The list could go on and on in favour of exercising and the only thing you could find against it is that, yes, it does take a bit of effort. But if none of the above key points appeals to you, all I will say to you is this: **this book isn't for you**!

There is a misconception that in order to improve your fitness you have to go through the pain barrier and half kill yourself. This is simply not true; all you have to do is elevate your heart rate for 30 or so minutes three times a week, to exercise the heart muscles. There are so many ways to do it these days, as every town or city has fitness centres catering for most sports, including tennis, badminton, aerobics, swimming and weight-training. Quite often people run their health by "crisis management" where, after a health scare, they then decide to look after themselves. Take my friend Ken; he was a hard-working manager at a chemical plant, often working long hours and then returning home to spend all his free time working on his home computer. Ken always said he had no time for exercising and had little inclination to do it. Whenever I brought up the subject of health it received little in the way of response. Ken was a smoker and didn't like to exercise. Then it happened; a heart attack. Ken was in shock. When he was taken to hospital and rested he noticed that all the other patients in the coronary care ward with him were over 20 years older than him! Needless to say, the experience changed his life and I am happy to say that Ken is now looking much better; he has stopped smoking and now enjoys his daily jogs on his home treadmill. The moral of the story is that many people have their heads in the sand when it comes to health and they try to bluff themselves into thinking that their health is O.K. when it isn't. It isn't O.K. to smoke, it isn't O.K. to be obese, and it isn't O.K. to be unfit. These things will catch up with you at some time or another and when they do you'd better have your will written out because the Grim Reaper's coming to see you! It's a lot better to help to avoid that scenario and begin to clean up your act. It's time to take responsibility for your health. Here's how:

1. You must join a gym or some kind of sports club. It's not good enough to say that you'll feel out of place because of the other, fitter people at the gym; it's not their fault if you are out of shape and don't look as good as them. Do not resent them; use them as motivation or a benchmark that you would like to aspire to yourself.

You must not think of the other people at the gym as your enemies; take some time to ask their advice on training tips. The first day is always the hardest but as you start to tone up and get fit you will start to enjoy going. Start to establish this as a habit, like brushing your teeth; it's just something that you do without thinking. For the fastest results in weight loss I recommend circuit training; this form of training is very tough but it sure helps to lose weight fast. When I did circuit training when I used to do boxing my weight dropped 20lbs in a month and I was as fit as a flea! Nowadays boxercise classes are run in most gyms; these are great for both men and women as they target the stomach and butt areas. Boxercise is also great for learning self-defence, as you never know when you might need it. Weight training is a must, too. I know of no other way to develop your body as quickly or effectively as weight training. You can literally sculpt your body by using specific exercises with weights to improve the areas that need the most attention very quickly.

You don't' get too old to exercise; you get old because you don't exercise.

There is plenty of free information about weight training either in libraries or from the staff at your local gyms. A mistake both men and women make often is that they think that if they lift weights they will grow muscles that are too big for them. This is a common misconception; ask any bodybuilder who is not on steroids if it is easy to build big muscles fast. Usually they will laugh at you and tell you that it takes years of dedicated training to build even a half-decent-sized body using weights. The effort to build big muscles is enormous and takes tons of food and very heavy weights unless you have the genetics of a Gorilla! I shake my head sometimes when I go down to my local gym and see people "exercising" on machines with so little resistance that they might as well not bother at all. You must train hard enough to get your heart rate elevated and sweat otherwise it won't do any good. I personally work out three days a week: one day with weights in the gym, another day with my home body weight resistance total body training bench, and the last one is boxercise training with or without a punch bag. Every day when I awake I do five minutes of stretching, I highly recommend this as it keeps you supple. And that's it; the total time spent training is three hours per week. In a week of 168 hours this equates to hardly anything, I still have 165 hours to do the rest! You will never find the time to work out; you have to make the time. Isn't it funny how people who have a heart attack suddenly find the time to work out afterwards?. Don't make excuses; make commitments. **Nothing** is more important than your health.

2. You must start to eat better. The food that you eat determines how well your body will work. Without the right balance of food types the body will soon weaken and become prone to disease. Without the right nutrients, like a car given the wrong fuel the body will develop major problems and start to fail you. When this happens often the damage from neglect has been too severe and then we look to doctors to save us. This is a crazy philosophy and is the characteristic of the reactive personality who never takes responsibility for his or her health. The nutrients from the food we eat are the coolants that we need to make the body's organs work properly and if this is neglected disease is a certainty. Unlike a car whose engine can simply be replaced, it is not so simple for us to change our hearts when they stop working — ask anybody who needs a transplant. Think about it this way: if you had a dog, would you feed your dog the same quality of food as the type that you eat? If not, why not? You might say "Of course not. I want my dog to be healthy and live a long life". Well, if you want the same for yourself, cut out the garbage and start respecting your body. If you put garbage into your system, the system will produce only garbage results. Start by cutting down on alcohol and drink it only on social occasions, **not** at home watching T.V. It is nothing more than a bad habit to have a drink every night and this must be greatly reduced if you want to live the best life ever. Alcohol dampens the mind. It is also a depressant so little progress can ever be made by the more than occasional drinker.

What we put into our bodies determines the output that we get. Put rubbish in and you will get rubbish out.

3. Take vitamins. There is much controversy when it comes to vitamin supplementation, with different experts saying different

things. Both sides of the argument have valid points and I have researched both viewpoints quite extensively. After studying both sets of data I have come to the resounding conclusion that not only do we need vitamin supplementation, but also without it we will probably die a lot sooner. I used to suffer quite badly from colds and flu but now I have found that if I take vitamin C when the first sign of a symptom begins, then it doesn't ever develop. In June 2000 I began taking Maximol Solutions which is a liquid colloidal vitamin and mineral supplement which I drink every day. There are over one hundred vitamins and trace minerals contained in sub-microscopic form in every daily intake. After three days of using this supplement I felt that my body had returned to my real age and that a new lease of life was upon me. As an expert on all things within the mind. I questioned whether the effects were due to my wanting this product to work and that the effects were merely a "placebo". To that I say this: one year on, I still feel exactly the same as I did after the first three days of taking the supplement. I now have an extra two hours a day of energy that I could not produce in the past, no matter how much I tried with positive thinking. I now am very rarely sick any more and if I am it is hardly worth mentioning. Recently I bumped into my G.P. who remarked on how well I looked and mentioned that he hadn't seen me in ages. To that I told him "I'm sorry, Doctor, but I don't think we will be seeing much of each other in the future!". At that he laughed and said to me that I should write a book (little did he know I had already started it!). Is it just a placebo effect that I feel? Maybe it is, but let me tell you this: if it is, I'll take the placebo any time rather than go back to the way I used to feel. Will I live to be over 100? Who knows if I will or not or whether I would have without supplementation or not? However I do know this for sure: however old I reach, I will definitely be making the most of my life. Regardless of how old I am before I depart, I know that I will be enjoying every moment with every up and down and I am committed to living the best life possible! You should too. I take two types of vitamin supplements, the first is Maximol Solutions , as mentioned above, available from www.neways.co.uk or for the U.S www.neways.com. The second is calcium in chelated form called "Calcium Bone Formula" from Kordells. Please note that I make no money from endorsing these products, nor do I work for these companies. These are just the products that I use and I tell it as it is. One of the of which I have recently become aware things while studying health is the importance of bodily pH in maintaining health. Experts say that for a person to be in good health and remain so their bodily pH should be around 7.4. What that means is that your saliva should be slightly alkaline and not acidic. Experts have found that when people become ill they predominantly have a pH that is acidic and not alkaline. This acidity can be destructive to our bodies as they try to compensate for this problem by extracting the necessary nutrients from our organs to try to correct our pH. Sometimes our bones are affected first as the calcium is extracted from them to bolster the deficit. Osteoporosis is the usual side-effect of this process. We must have the correct bodily pH in order for us to remain healthy and disease-free. A simple way to test your own pH is to take a litmus paper test. This paper can be bought at some chemists or it can be ordered. By dipping some litmus paper into the saliva in your mouth you will get an instant result of your bodily pH (hopefully around 7.4). The test should come back blue unless you have a different colour of litmus paper; some testing kits have the pH scale on the product itself. I would definitely invest in such a kit for your own peace of mind. The last kit I bought cost around £5 and I have done over 200 tests with it! Experts say that in order to change bodily pH, supplements are invaluable, Calcium is one element that when used a s a supplement helps to correct your pH. A friend of mine started on the same supplementation as myself and in six months his pH went from 6.0 acidic to 7.4 alkaline. Do not expect rapid results from supplements, though, as they do not work like drugs. For more in depth information on pH and its role in health I recommend *The Calcium Factor* by Robert R. Barefoot and Carl J. Reich, M.D. (ISBN 0-9633703-3-2-4).

4. You must master your mind. The very thoughts that we think can influence bodily pH as a person who thinks negatively will release adrenalin into his or her bloodstream which can seriously affect the body's organs. Adrenalin in small doses is quite healthy but in large amounts, as occur when people are very stressed all the time it is very dangerous. Ulcers and heart disease are common symptoms of stress, which can be caused by our negative thinking. Every time you get annoyed or stressed your body releases adrenalin, which

begins to attack your bodily organs and then also affects your pH. It is vital that you learn not to over-react when you find yourself in difficult situations. This can be done by closing your eyes and mentally reviewing a past situation where you became stressed or annoyed, and then imagine the scenario with a different ending. Imagine yourself reacting to the situation in a calm, confident manner and run the scenario through in your mind, just as if you were running a movie. When you've run it through a few times, ask yourself if you're happy with the new way you handled it. If you are, **decide** to use this option next time a similar situation arises. When you do this your mind now has a memory of this new way of doing things, so it will select this new, better way of behaving next time a similar situation arises. Simple, yet very effective.

5. Don't be a moaner. Isn't it funny how people who moan a lot usually have poorer health than people who don't? They constantly moan about their health and their lives and they get worse and worse the more they moan. What they have failed to learn is that their thoughts have actually contributed to their physical health and the more they moan and get annoyed about it, the worse they get. With every moan and every gripe, more and more adrenalin is being flushed into the body, which then attacks the organs and alters the pH. This person **must** change their thoughts because their thoughts are actually killing them! Moaning continuously about this or that is merely a bad habit that needs to be stopped — and it **can** be very simply, by making a decision to do so. So some form of relaxation is needed. There are lots of different ways we can do this but I'm going to show you the way I do it, which is simple, effective and fast. Don't worry if you find using your imagination a little difficult, as it becomes easier with practice.

In the following exercise I ask you to think about a relaxing scene which is pleasant. This can be a real place or an imagined, fantasy destination. The more you can vividly imagine your place of relaxation, the more relaxed you will feel. At first glance it may look too simple but don't be put off; the total time to achieve the relaxed state is about three minutes. The only real things that you have to do are sit, breathe, look, hear, and picture the way you would be looking if you felt totally relaxed. Do not be put off by the simplicity of this relaxation induction; it can be used when time is not on your side and you need a quick boost. Please take the time actually to go through this process otherwise it is nothing more than words written in a book, which will not manifest into anything and will be easily forgotten. Put this book down **now** and do it!

Because our thoughts control our feelings, we need only relax and think pleasant thoughts in order to receive pleasant feelings.

Quick Relax

1. **Find a comfortable chair or lie down on your bed.**
2. **Take three big deep breaths and exhale slowly with each one.**
3. **Sit or lie down in the way you would do if you felt totally relaxed.**
4. **Breathe in the manner that you would do if you felt totally relaxed.**
5. **Make your face look the way it would if you felt totally relaxed.**
6. **Hear the things that you would hear if you felt totally relaxed.**
7. **Picture the things that you would see if you felt totally relaxed. This can be anything that you wish: a beach, the countryside, or your own private fantasy!**
8. **Become fully absorbed with this scene and deepen your state with suggestions if required.**

Stay young

A great quote regarding age comes from Dr Wayne Dyer. Wayne simply says:

"Don't let an old person take over your body".

I love this quote and I always use it with my clients. What it means is that you have to remember to stay young. You must use the mindset of not beginning to the think of yourself as somebody who is getting older every day. Grow up but don't get old. Growing up has nothing to do with age; it's about growing and maturing as a person. I see a lot of clients on a weekly basis who, despite the fact that they are older than me, are still immature. They still make the same childish bad decisions and do the same childish things that they have been doing since they **were** children. When we mature we are working with our inner wisdom as guidance and we have the ability to transcend the silly traits that we used to do out of habit. I know people who are the same age as myself but say the same things that I hear much older and cantankerous people say. At what age do you have to start buying dull, boring clothes? At what age do you start moaning about life? These things don't have to start at all. As we said in the chapter on beliefs, what you believe becomes a self-fulfilling prophecy, so if you believe that you're getting old, that belief will begin to manifest into a physical reality! If you believe that when we get older we start to stiffen up and become less mobile then we will begin to make those provisions within ourselves and stop stretching our muscles. If you think that as you get older you have to get very serious about life and watch the news and get very cynical about life then all this will start to become your reality too.

Age is a concept; how fast you age depends on whose concept you have bought into.

Let me ask you a question: Are you really ready to be old, or do you still want to live a young life? Who decides at what point we age? There are certain stereotypes that a lot of people buy into. Let me give you an example:

At 21 we become an adult and start to lose our youthful attitude. At 30 we begin to "settle down" and start to become more mature, forgetting silly, youthful exuberance and starting to think about the "real issues". At 40 we start to gain weight as the "inevitable" middle age spread starts to show and we start thinking about our retirement. At 50 we now know all about our physical limitations and take it easy, maybe gaining an extra 20lbs. At this point we start to use the past as a yardstick and we begin to moan that life was better back then, before all this new technology came along. At 60 we have either been given early retirement or more probably have been out of work for some time because of the fact that we "couldn't adapt" to the change in modern working practices. At 60+ plus we wait for old age **really** to set in, waiting for arthritis or Alzheimer's disease to occur. How does this sound? Do you want to be a part of that? If your answer is "Yes", I wish you well but if your answer is "No", well, let's have some fun!

Don't buy into that "As you get older, things start to get harder to learn" rubbish. And don't have the attitude that all the fast-growing technology is too much for your brain. Scientists haven't begun to scratch the surface of how powerful our minds are and even now they estimate that we only use about 10 per cent of it! Our minds are adapting brilliantly to the new technology that is changing on a weekly basis and there is still much more to come. In fact, there is a lot more to come because what we might believe now is the height of technological growth will seem ancient in just a few years. Instead of fearing change, think "Bring it on!" because the hard drive of your mind can never be filled as it expands with every new change we encounter. Think of the luxuries we have at home right now, such as T.V. We could never give them back now because we are **used** to them. Don't fall behind the game; stay ahead of it. Don't worry — you **can** handle it, in fact you **need** it. If our minds are not being stimulated with new and varied bits of information (no, not what's going on in your favourite soap opera), they will create problems to give us a bit of "drama". For instance, if you retire early from work, where before you had a busy physical and mental workload, sometimes the mind will give you a problem in order to give you something to think about. Weird, huh? It's like the bored child who starts playing with matches and then sets a toy on fire. The bored brain needs stimulation. This is especially relevant to the more elderly among us, as too much time at home thinking can be counter-productive. Unfortunately, the best some retired people can come up with is tending the garden. I'm sorry, but that won't cut it; stimulation has to come from new and unexplored stuff. For some reason, if the mind is not stimulated with new and varied activities and information we run the risk of becoming a moaner and general grump.

When the mind gets bored it will create something to make you think about. Sometimes it's good but mostly it's bad.

Where I live quite a high percentage of my neighbours are elderly people. Every day I see them walking around with their mouths turned down as they meet each other in the street to moan about the world. I see them agreeing with each other, seeking validation for their negative beliefs and wanting to be proved right. These types of people are like an infection; if you give them ten minutes of your precious time they will leave you feeling depressed and down. Is it any wonder that nobody wants to visit them? I was talking to a guy the other day who was complaining that nobody from his family ever visits him any more. This guy was such a negative drag that I couldn't wait to get away from him either!

O.K., what's my point?

We must be careful as we get older that we do not fall into the moaning trap. It is too easy to read and believe everything we see in the papers and start to complain about it. Instead of moaning about it, why not do something about it? Moaning never solved anything.

You must give your mind plenty of <u>good</u> stimulation and you must be committed to gaining further knowledge. Knowledge is the key to personal growth. The pursuit of knowledge is the key to happiness and fulfilment because when we are not learning we can start thinking too much and become too inwardly focused. Thinking about ourselves too much can be counter-productive, because the bored mind starts to find faults in our life. Knowledge and the pursuit of it is the life-blood that excites us and makes our lives fulfilling. Without it we become drawn into a hum-drum life without challenge.

"Unless you try to do something beyond what you have already mastered, you will never grow."

Anon

Remember that the conscious mind is the enemy of inner peace and using the conscious mind for our everyday thinking is a recipe for mental anguish! Whenever a person relies on the conscious mind for direction and enlightenment in life they are literally on a crash course into despair. It's amazing when the clients I see begin to understand the principles and start to notice the differences of the two minds, how fast they adapt to using their wise inner mind. Usually at first when I tell people about the two minds and explain the differences I am faced with scepticism. Now, though, I can tell instantly those who are conscious mind-directed and those who are subconscious wisdom-directed, just by the conversations we have in therapy. It's amazing when, in a short time, clients come into my office and start to talk and think wisely for maybe the first time in years. The difference is **mind-blowing**!

Quite often when clients come into my office they are very emotional, which is a characteristic of the conscious mind thinker. With all that conscious mind babble going on in their heads, they are unable to come up with anything of any sense and are often confused. We must move away from the use of the conscious mind for direction as it will cause only misery. The more we rely on it as we get older, the more confused and cantankerous we will become. We all know people like this who are a nightmare to be around. They get quite upset and dramatic over every little thing and blow it **waaaaaaaayyyyyyy** out of proportion. Quite often a client will come to see me and as soon as they sit down they will burst into tears and get dramatic as they tell me about the "terrible week" they have had. Usually, though, the week wasn't as terrible as the person might have first thought. Mostly the upset was caused by blowing things out of proportion and letting the chatter of the conscious mind wind them up. Have you ever had the experience of thinking that some awful consequence was going to occur and got really upset only to find later that things weren't as bad as you first thought and then afterwards you felt embarrassed about the way you acted? Have you ever had the experience of speaking to somebody who is nearly hysterical explain to you in great detail something that they feel is negative, and you thought "What's the big deal?".

When we focus on the negative events of our lives the tendency is to blow them way out of proportion. It is wise then to relax regularly, to stop the conscious mind from exaggerating the truth.

Think of a mini crisis that you once had to deal with in your life and remember how upset you become. Now that it is over, was it as bad as you once thought it to be? It's funny how, quite often, when we get worked up over something and think it's the end of our world, maybe a day or a week later it fades away into insignificance. Reacting in an over-the-top manner to every difficulty in life is the characteristic of the conscious mind thinker. Behaving like a dramatic actor whenever we are faced with a difficulty is a common trait in such people, often bursting into tears whenever something goes wrong or ranting like a madman when things are not going the way they planned. This type of childish behaviour, once learned and repeated, quickly becomes a habit so that every difficulty is dealt with in the same stupid way. If you find yourself over-reacting on a regular basis you need to read this next bit very carefully.

Whenever a person over-reacts it is because that person is not using their wisdom to guide them. If they were, their wisdom would not say to them "Start to rant and rave". Instead, whenever you are faced by a situation where in the past you acted in a way that you were later embarrassed about or you said something that you didn't mean you, should always pause for a couple of seconds. This gives a little time for your wisdom to step in as your wisdom tends to be a bit slower than your conscious mind, which instantly tells you to react. This process of pausing briefly is a simple and very effective way of preventing things that you may regret afterwards. This gives the subconscious wisdom time to think of an appropriate response.

It is important to understand that our behaviours that we don't like **don't** have to be with us forever, nor are they genetic. Plenty of times I have heard people blaming the family that they grew up with for their behaviours. Behaviours can be changed, and changed easily, once you know how to do it. Use this simply exercise as many times as needed to change **your** unwanted behaviours. Some people find it useful to record the next exercise on a tape, giving the appropriate pauses when necessary to allow time for the mental changes to take place. This way you can concentrate on doing the exercise and not on trying to remember each step. Feel free to adapt the above script for your own personal circumstances — as long as it works for you, it doesn't matter.

Further information about the application of the action signals process can be found by purchasing Anthony Robbins' *Lessons In Mastery* home study course, available at most good stockists.

Unwanted Social Behaviour Change Exercise

1. **Before such an incident occurs, where in the past you have behaved in an over-the-top manner, review some of these past regrettable experiences like small movies in your mind and ask yourself this question "How would I like to act instead of this?".**

2. **Begin to run a movie in your mind with yourself behaving in ways in which you would prefer to behave instead. As you begin to run that movie, notice the distinctions in your behaviour that brought about a different outcome.**

3. **Note all the differences in your behaviour and keep them in mind. Ask yourself "What did I do differently?" and note the changes.**

4. **Make a decision to try these new behaviours the next time you are faced with a similar situation.**

5. **After a real situation has happened where you tried out your new behaviour, review it and, when you are relaxed, perhaps fine-tune it mentally, with more visualisation if needed.**

6. **If the outcome was better than it used to be, give yourself a pat on the back and decide to keep the new approach. Now that you have more choices in how to behave, your subconscious mind will use the best way rather than the only way. You have now taken a positive step to change your unwanted behaviours. Repeat as necessary.**

Chapter Five

Principle 5: Remember — Happiness is a STATE

What does "Happiness is a state" mean? Let me tell you first of all that the type of state I am talking about is **not** the type of state you may find yourself in when you leave your local pub! What I am talking about is the state of mind and body that is needed in order to keep us happy. We have already learned in the previous chapters that our minds and how we think affect the way we feel but what I would like to do now is talk about how we can use our bodies to influence the way we feel too. Our bodies and how we use them have a very powerful effect on how we feel. The posture that we use and how we breathe can affect us positively or negatively, depending on how we use them. This simple fact cannot be taken lightly as the effect it has on us can be quite dramatic.

Whenever we use our posture and breathing in certain ways, our bodies send signals to our brains that tell us how to think. These signals become conditioned in time and then become an automatic response whenever we use the same posture and breathing. Whenever we are confident, sad, depressed or excited we adopt the posture and breathing to support that feeling. Every time we adopt a certain posture according to whatever we are feeling this then becomes a conditioned response. So, no matter how you feel, when you change your posture and breathing into the one that has been conditioned, you will always get the same conditioned response. Let's say, for instance, that when you were younger you used to suffer from depression. During those depressed times you would always adopt a posture and breathing style to reflect the mood you were in. Every time you did this, it then became coded into your body and then into your mind so that this posture and breathing meant that you were depressed. The problem is that from now on, whenever you use the same posture or breathing, your body sends a signal to your brain and tells you that you are depressed.

You could be sitting there feeling O.K. one minute and then for no reason you could begin to feel depressed. What has happened? Your body has remembered the posture and breathing code and sent it to your brain for analysis. Once this process starts, the whole analysis thing can begin and the "Why?" question comes into play, which is counter-productive for your happiness. You must begin to understand that this body-to-mind combination is a powerful force, which must not be underestimated. The good news, though, is that we can use this to our advantage if we so wish.

To master your state is to have ultimate power over your emotions. Do this and you can have confidence on tap whenever you need it.

Whenever people come into my office I can usually see what the problem is by the posture they use. The stressed out individuals who come to see me adopt a rather edgy physiology and sit on the edge of the seat. They look uptight and have tense facial muscles, they breathe quickly and in a shallow manner, as if air were restricted somehow. When they speak they speak quickly, as if they are in a hurry, and their tonality is sharp and to the point. Whenever people come in suffering from depression this also reflects in their posture. They usually have a certain facial expression and tonality to match. When people come to see me complaining of lack of self-confidence they tend to make themselves smaller physically than what they actually are, by looking down and speaking quietly. These common complaints can quickly be changed for the better by understanding and using the following knowledge.

When I first heard about this body-to-mind connection and its effects on our mental state, I was sceptical. Back in the days of being a novice trying to build my self-confidence, I tried lots of different ways to do just that. I tried positive self-talk, self-hypnosis, subliminal messages and just about everything else that was being touted around back then. Nothing was as powerful as what I am going to present to you next. The only problem that you may find with it is that it is so easy that you might not believe it! Please keep an open mind as to the potential of the following information as it accounts for roughly 50% of self-confidence.

In the same way that we have codes for negative stuff like depression we also have inside us the codes for self-confidence and happiness. We just have to find them. Here's the good news: if you had only one time in your life where you experienced self confidence, that time was coded from your posture and imprinted into your nervous system. What this means is that if you ever want to call upon your confidence, all you have to do is find your code. Your code is a special posture and breathing combination with facial expression that when used them simultaneously will make you feel tremendously confident and unstoppable. This confident state can then be called upon whenever you need it, by just accessing the right sequences. This has to be tried to be believed. The only thing that could stop it from working is if you don't really try to do it properly and tell yourself that it won't work. It does work, and it works brilliantly. You just have to practise a bit in order to find your code. Lack of self-confidence is one of the most common things people say that they would like to improve upon as it can manifest itself in lots of different forms, such as shyness, stammering, avoiding meeting new people, job interviews and anything else that people avoid. Most people are not aware that their posture and breathing could have such a powerful effect on their lives. The best thing of all is that when you change into your position of confidence something magical occurs. It changes the way that you **think** automatically. Yes, that's right: it does it for you as it sends a different signal to your mind which changes the way you feel. Have you noticed that when you are in your posture of **no confidence**, the little voice inside your head tells you all the nasty, negative stuff that you don't really want to hear? O.K., then let's cut to the chase and begin to use this knowledge for some good. Below is a model for finding your codes and changing the way that you feel. I have used the example of self-confidence to show how to use this knowledge effectively, although any state you wish could have been used.

How to Access YOUR Most Resourceful States

This process is the **key** to living the type of life you want. By using the body's own posture codes, we are able to bring about any state (positive or negative) we wish. By using these codes we are able to tap into whatever state of being we want — instantly! You see, happiness, unhappiness, confidence, joy, assertiveness and tranquillity are not things that just happen to us. They are **states of being**. Use this simple process next to unlock your codes so that these states of being can be called upon at any time.

1. **Decide what state you desire (for example, confidence).**
2. **Sit or stand in the way you would stand if you felt totally and completely confident (change your posture).**
3. **Breathe in the way you would breathe if you felt totally and completely confident.**
4. **Make your face look how it would look if you felt totally and completely confident. Talk and sound that way.**
5. **Hear the things in your own mind that you would hear if you felt totally and completely confident.**
6. **Remember the time(s) when you felt self-confident and re-create the same feelings that you had back then through your thoughts and enjoy feeling this way. Remember this feeling.**
7. **Stand or sit that way, breathe that way, look that way, hear that way, smile and enjoy the feelings that you have created.**

If you have run through this exercise properly, you should feel very confident right now. If you don't, it's because you are telling yourself that what you are doing is dumb or that it won't work. It **will** work. Try it again and do it properly this time! If you can't think of a time, imagine how you **think** you would look, stand, breath, etc. When you have the feeling you desire, you have found the **code** for that resource so that in the future when you need that resource you simply go through these steps! The change of **posture** is the biggest factor for changing your state. When you're depressed you adopt a posture of depression and that triggers the code for unhappiness; change your posture and you will change your state. Use this **consistently** in your life and you'll be **amazed** by how much more confident you will feel. Self-confidence is around 50 per cent physiology and 50 per cent mindset, so not to use it would be crazy!

We use different postures to create the different moods we have. If you want to be in a better mood, choose a better posture.

Let me show you how I use this gift in helping myself in my public speaking seminars. One time I was due to speak to a group of top-flight businessmen. I had been told prior to the seminar that all the guys had seen it, done it and bought the T-shirt when it came to personal development and that I'd "better be good". This did not faze me at all. In fact, the more the odds are stacked against me, the more I enjoy turning the situation around. It would have been easy to slip into a posture of terror but I decided that I wanted to do a great job so I went into my state for confidence. I had only one and a half days to practise the whole thing because I had been called in on very short notice so I practised the whole routine in my position of confidence which, for me, meant shoulders back, arms around my back, breathing deeply and fully, so as not to restrict my air supply, and having a look of total confidence on my face. The beauty of doing this is that it changes the little voice in your head, automatically. The voice does not say those negative things to you any more; in fact, just the opposite. The day of the seminar came and I was faced with 20 or so businessmen of various ages and different demeanours. I was introduced with "This is Steve Norton who is a personal development trainer and if he is garbage we will never hire him again". This was not really the introduction that I was looking for, but because I was in my position of confidence it didn't faze me. I gave a good seminar and they all said they enjoyed it. Without this knowledge of the confidence codes I could very easily have crumpled into a "loser's" posture. Nothing they could have said could have affected my performance that day as, once you find your code and use it; it then begins to act like a shield.

Try this: stand in the way that you would stand if you had **no** self-confidence. Go through the breathing changes and facial expressions that you would have if you had no self-confidence. You can also do this sitting down if you want, as it makes no difference, but please do this. Let me ask you a question: how is the little voice inside your head sounding? Is it just the same or is it now more negative? For 99 per cent of people it would have become more negative, and you may have started to feel a little "down". Now try this: switch into your position of confidence and go through the breathing change and facial expression change and notice whether the little voice inside your head has changed. If you have done this properly and with the right effort you should find that the little voice inside your head is now more positive. You should feel better and more assertive, more powerful and able to take charge of any situation. If this is not how you feel then you haven't found your code yet. You may need to practise this in front of a mirror a few times before you find your code, and then begin to use it consistently whenever you want to feel confident. In fact, why not use it all the time? The more you use it; the more you make it a habit.

Let's take some examples of two real cases that I have dealt with. I have changed the names but the facts are correct. The first one involved Bill. Bill was a charismatic character who came to me complaining that he'd lost his self-confidence. This was a genuinely funny guy who for years had had the job of chairman at a local gentlemen's club. His job was to address the members and speak for a short while about the various aspects of the meeting. For years he had done a fine job but for some reason unknown to him he had started to get nervous and have panic attacks. This really bothered him as people had started to mention it to him. I said to him: "What are you doing differently now compared to what you were doing before, when you had lots of confidence?". To that he replied: "I don't know. I think I'm doing the same things." Then I said: "Stand the way you stand now whenever you give a speech. Look that way, breathe that way and sound that way." He stood up and changed his posture into his usual physiology when speaking and he looked miserable. When he spoke he had no conviction in his voice and he started to fiddle with his hands at the front. I could see the confidence draining away from his body and he looked uncomfortable. Then I said: "O.K., Bill, stand the way that you **used** to stand when you were confident." Straight away he changed his posture, with his hands around his back, smiling and relaxed. He started to breathe more deeply and easily and, when I asked him to speak, he spoke with a true resonance in his voice. He said he felt marvellous and reported that he was thinking more confidently. I told him to remember this code and to use it for the meeting the following night. A week later Bill came back to my office looking a lot more relaxed. He told me that he hadn't given as good a performance as that in years, and he said that people were saying how good he had been. The difference was that he wasn't even nervous when he stood up and he was only excited which is a normal feeling when we do things like public speaking. He was delighted and said that somebody came to see him afterwards to shake his hand with admiration. I told him that in the future when he needed that same confidence boost all he had to do was use the position of confidence again. I told him that if he lost it again, it would be down to not using his confidence code and **not** to losing his self-confidence. I did **nothing** other than help Bill to learn how to change his physiology and find his confidence code and the rest just fell into place.

Another case that I dealt with was that of a young man who had lost his confidence after being mugged. Let's call him Robert. Robert came to see me, saying that he was afraid of going out at night and that this was severely handicapping his life. When we went through the posture check we found that the posture he was using was the physiology of a victim. He had unwittingly adopted a victim posture, breathing and facial expression. He would walk with his head down, avoiding eye contact with anybody, and this would signal to his brain that he was scared. Also it made him feel weak and made him appear so. I said to him: "I want you to stand the way that you would be standing if you felt totally self-confident", and he did. We went through the breathing change and changing his facial expression to one more confident-looking. I had also noticed that he had been using a victim tonality in his voice so we got him to raise the volume up one notch. Immediately he felt better and left with the new-found knowledge of his bodily codes firmly in his mind, promising to use it for a week. The following week he returned like a new man and, although still a little wary, he was feeling much better. A couple of sessions later he felt confident enough to be able to do again all the things that he used to be afraid of.

I have taught this very simple technique to lots of people who claim to have "lost" their confidence, and gained similar results. The only challenge that people have when they try the confidence code technique, or even when they read about it, is that it is so simple they do not believe that it could work!

Is this used solely for gaining self-confidence?

Absolutely not. The only limits to this are those of your imagination. Every state that you could possibly want can be replicated and used by you in this way. This is great news because whatever we **want** to feel we **can** feel, simply by finding the right code. Every state you could ever want is there at your disposal because even if you have experienced the feeling only once, that code is locked into your body and your mind, ready for you to tap into. It even works if you pretend.

Have you ever noticed how sometimes your memory seems worse than at other times? How sometimes things seem to go in one ear and out of the other? This is because you are in the posture of **not** learning. Maybe you are slumped or are resting your head on your hand. Your body recognises this to be the physiology of boredom so that whatever you are listening to or reading goes straight in and out the other side. There have been other times, though, when you have learned things quickly and easily and you have still remembered those things to this very day. This is because you were in the right posture and physiology to do that and you weren't slumped over, looking bored. So with this knowledge we can control our memory retention rate to make it more powerful too. Whenever we need to learn something, all we have to do is find our code for doing just that and use it. This gives us the edge over those who don't know this technique but that's tough for them: they should have bought this book just as you had the good sense to do!

Using this knowledge, we are able to find any state we wish to be in, including:

Peaceful; Tranquil; Assertive; Relaxed; Happy; Carefree; Strong and Powerful; Empathetic; Intelligent; Super-confident; Curious; Motivated; Loving; Content.

In fact, any state you wish to be in you can have, simply by going through the steps outlined earlier in the section Accessing Your Most Resourceful States Technique. The good news is that you don't have to go to Tibet in order to find inner peace; you can have it in your own home.

Some people might say that when you do this you are only faking it. To that I say: **no way**. When you use this technique you will genuinely change the way you feel. Just because you wake up in a ratty mood it doesn't mean that you have to stay in that state all day. If you know how to change it, it would be dumb not to use that knowledge. Some days I wake up and feel "down". If somebody in the street asks me how I'm doing I will always reply "Fantastic" or "Brilliant", even if I don't feel this way. Why? Because if I say "Well, you know, I really feel awful" and then begin to bore somebody half to death with my tales of woe I will make them feel bad and make myself feel worse. Even if I fake it, it still feels better to say that I feel "Brilliant" than to say "I feel awful". The language that you use to describe the way you feel has a direct effect on how you feel as it too has been coded into certain feelings by your conditioning of it.

Power up your tonality

The story behind this simple phrase is something about which I feel quite strongly. Every day I meet people whose tonality is so bad that they repel others. Some people adopt a dull, monotonous tone, which makes people switch off from them even if what they are saying might actually be interesting. People with dull, boring tonalities usually have dull, boring lives to match. When people are depressed their tonality tends to reflect their mood and, even if they aren't depressed, using a dull tonality will get them there in the end. It's also the tone of choice of the loser and the person who has a rather negative outlook on life. They tend to say negative statements like "What's the point? It's going to rain anyway, it always does on my day off" and similar statements. The tonality that we use has a direct effect on the way that we feel. It is no surprise, then, to understand that when people are generally happy they have a happy, upbeat tonality to match. They always sound positive regardless of what's going on and are rarely fazed when difficulties occur. "What doesn't kill me makes me stronger" is the motto of this personality type. The negative thinker, on the other hand, usually has a very boring, monotonous voice that has negative undertones within it. When they speak their words are used with negative tones to try to get some kind of agreement from you regarding whatever concepts they are trying to get you to buy into.

If you've got something to say, say it with confidence, say it loud enough and say it with clarity.

All the time I hear people with negative tonalities talking together in their monotonous tones, slagging off the world and pulling it apart. They agree with one another and seem to get some kind of sad satisfaction at being "proved right" whenever something negative happens. Over the years I have never met any person with bad tonality who ever become successful or truly happy. They tend to be the moaners of the world, the downers and the unhappiest. In fact the only time they appear to be happy is when something bad happens and then they can say "I told you so". They seek to be proved right in their negative beliefs and are not interested in a different viewpoint. Even bad tonality on the telephone is a common problem, with people speaking apathetically to each other. If you think that you have such a tonality, here is the good news. With a little practice you can very easily change your voice tone into something more positive and uplifting. If your voice tone puts people to sleep you have two choices: you could either train to be a hypnotist or change your tone by practice. The type of voice tone you have will determine how successful you are at making friends, how much money you will make, how successful you are with the opposite sex and how happy you will feel. So it's very important that you have good tonality and begin to practise improving it. I find that people who say that they are unconfident tend to talk too quietly, as if what they are saying is not really important, and they usually think that people aren't really interested in what they have to say anyway. When you speak too quietly the message that you send out is that what you are saying actually isn't that important, and that people don't really have to listen to what you have to say. You might as well be saying "You can butt in whenever you feel free". This happens quite frequently to people who speak too quietly; they get interrupted all the time because their voice portrays weakness to the other person's more "dominant" personality.

Do not be afraid to turn up the volume of your voice. You may feel a little self-conscious when you first try this but in time you will be delighted by the influence and personal power that you will gain from using it. It will not be as obvious as you might think, because you only have to turn the volume knob up a little bit to make a big difference. As long as you don't start shouting, then it's O.K.! Practising and testing this out is the key to successful and confident speaking. Practise different voice modulations daily to begin to perfect it. A person with more flexibility in their voice tone will have greater power to influence and get what they want.

One of the things that I have learned to do since my training is to vary my tonality, my accent and the volume of my voice to suit whatever environment I am in. The power to influence people by using voice tone is a skill that is understood and used by the successful person but rarely realised by the shy person. The average person usually does not realise the power of "**how** we say" rather than "**what** we say" in its effect with regard to persuasion. Whenever I talk to somebody I mentally gauge them and adapt my tonality and accent to suit. If I think they are having a bad day I will not try to cheer them up with a big grin and positive tonality, but instead I will match their tonality and use my persuasion skills to bring them round to my way of thinking. If I know that a person has a generally warm and happy personality then I will greet them in the same way. This builds rapport.

A quick guide on how to build rapport

The reason why we want to build rapport is that we want to get along with people and influence them. Without those skills it is very difficult to get ahead or gain any ground. It is very hard to build strong relationships with partners, friends or colleagues if you don't know how to gain rapport. Some people have the ability to have rapport with anybody while others struggle. The naturally good rapport makers are often blissfully unaware of their skill and perhaps do not know why people like them.

Through time, the components of how to gain rapport have been broken down and many models have been made from them. The idea is that if you use this knowledge and apply those same components you will be able to gain rapport with anybody. This is very true as I have used these models myself when working with clients, with whom having rapport is essential if we are to work together. The models that are generally used, although good, in my experience are not without exceptions to the rules. As with anything in life, things don't always work out the way we expect them to. That is why, in time, I have found myself moving away from the usual models of rapport and relying more on my intuition.

The standard model for building rapport acknowledges that **what** we say accounts for only 7 per cent of how we are perceived. The next chunk of rapport is our tonality, or **how** we say things, which accounts for 38 per cent. And the final chunk is body language, which makes up the final 55 per cent. Most people are surprised when they find out that "**what** we say" amounts to only about 7 per cent. Most people think that what we say is the vital component for getting on with people, when in fact it is the **least important**. The words themselves mean very little if our voice, tone and body language are not congruent with what we are trying to say. If you were to say "I love you" but then said it in a dull, unfeeling manner then the person hearing it would not believe it.

Communication is everything. Without it, we don't get ahead. Sell yourself through your communication.

People go to great lengths to emphasise their words carefully when trying to influence people and more often than not they come away unsuccessful. There are various reasons behind this. One of the reasons that we have found is that people tend to be inclined to think out of one of three sensory modes:

- **auditory (hearing);**
- **visual (sight); or**
- **kinesthetic (feelings).**

Although we have five senses, the majority of people tend to use these three modes most, the other two sensory modes being gustatory (taste) and olfactory (smell). We use all our senses but we tend to use one of them more predominantly to help us map our world. There is no right or wrong sensory mode to have; it's just what we use to make sense of our lives. Quite often the clues to which sensory mode we are using comes out in our every day communications.

The person who is predominantly a **visual** thinker will say things such as:

"It's nice to see you."
"It doesn't look right to me."
"Can you imagine that?"
"The future's looking bright."
"Picture this."
"Show me what you mean."
"It appears to me … "

They tend to use words that are visually-related, such as "**see**", "**look**", "**picture**", "**visualise**", "**image**", "**focus**", "**scene**", "**watch**", "**notice**", "**outlook**", "**reveal**", "**show**", and any other visual wordings. This person tends to speak quite quickly and gestures with their hands to "show" what they mean.

The person who is predominantly an auditory thinker will say things such as:

"I don't like the sound of that."
"It doesn't ring a bell."
"I'm hearing it loud and clear."
"Listen to me."
"I want to sound out that idea first."
"Let me tell you."
"It's music to my ears."

These types tend to use words that have an auditory connection, such as "**hear**", "**sound**", "**rings**", "**listen**", "**tone**", "**resonate**", "**monotonous**", "**vocal**", and any other auditory wordings. This person tends to talk a little more slowly and "listens" to what you say.

The person who is predominately a kinesthetic thinker will say things such as:

"It doesn't feel right to me."
"He rubs me up the wrong way."
"She gives me the chills."
"I was touched by it."
"I shiver at the thought."
"I can't put my finger on it."
"I felt it in my bones."

These types tend to use words that have a feeling connection, such as "**grasp**", "**hold**", "**catch**", "**feel**", "**touching**", "**skin**", "**handle**", "**rub**", "**hot/cold**", "**gentle**", "**smooth**", and any other kinesthetic wordings. Usually this person talks very slowly, sometimes too slowly for some people who want to speed them up!

The other two lesser-used senses — smell and taste — are not usually dominant senses and this is why I have not highlighted their presence so much.

Why is knowing this information useful?

It is useful to know what modes we use predominantly so that we can become aware of the language patterns of others and ourselves. This can be invaluable when we need to get our ideas across with the least amount of resistance. If we try to **voice** our ideas to another person with an opposite sensory mode to ours it could fall on **deaf ears**. Do you **see** what I mean?

Whenever we try to communicate with people who have different sensory modes than our own it is important to know that they will find it hard to trust us if we are not using the same sensory mode as them. Even if what you have to say is a valid, intelligent point, it could still be dismissed by the person with whom you want to impress it, because of the different sensory modes that you use.

To find out which sensory mode you use, think about this. Do you like art and going to the cinema? Are you good at visualising and using your imagination? Do you have to see ideas take shape? Or are you influenced by music; does it change your mood? Do you have an expensive hi-fi? Or does the sound of a person's voice and the tonality make you feel at ease with them or not? Does it have to sound good to you before you buy it? Or do you have to feel right before you buy something? Do you have to get a feeling about somebody before you trust them? Do you get emotional quite often? Do you like to cuddle/hold hands a lot? Of course we all use some of the above from time to time but there is usually one that is used more predominantly by us than the rest. Give it some thought. I myself am predominantly an auditory thinker and I can be sold anything if you have a pleasant voice! Music has a big effect on me and I always wake up to it. In fact, now, as I am writing, I am relaxed, listening to music. I am very aware of a person's tonality when communicating and I vary my own tonality often to suit the situation. What I have found, though, is now that I understand sensory modes and their effect on others I use a broader range of senses. With this information you can begin to use all of your senses more and not only your predominant one.

People like people who are like themselves

Yes, folks, it's true; we like people who are just like us. We tend to get on with people who think like us, sound like us and act like us. Whenever we are with people like this, we feel a special connection — a bond — and we trust them. This is the essence of rapport. Without this knowledge mismatches often occur when two different modes try to reach agreement. So if you want to gain rapport with more people you have to go first. It is unlikely that the person with whom you are communicating will have this knowledge and they will talk to you without noticing your different sensory modes. If the person with whom you want to gain rapport happens to be your boss then it is vital that you put this knowledge to use. By matching the other person's sensory mode and speaking through their mental sensory filter we are able to get along with people who might have normally dismissed us. You will be amazed how effective this is. You have to practise, though, and that means that you have to be pretty aware and switched on with this in order for it to work. Also, matching a person's "key words" is another great tool that I use, which brings about instant rapport. It is essential, however, that you don't overdo it because if they suspect you are doing it, it will bring about a break in rapport.

I once met a business manager once who used the word "dovetail" in his sentences all the time. All I had to do was say it a couple of times in my sentences and we were getting along like two old friends! Whenever I see a client I ask what profession they are in. If they are a mechanic I will talk about therapy as if I were talking about fixing a car: " We're going to **fine-tune** your mind" or " Get to the **nuts and bolts**". Or if the person were a financial consultant we would "**ensure** that change is quick and easy" and "use a **policy** of confidence-building". The possibilities are endless with this; all you have to do is experiment. You can "**build** bridges" with builders or "get to the **heart** of the matter" with doctors; the choice is up to you. Do not be put off by the simplicity of this knowledge; practise this and you will become a very popular person indeed.

The next stage for gaining rapport is matching the other person's **tonality**. If the person with whom you are communicating has a quick rate of speech, you must speed yours up to match theirs if you want to gain their trust. Have you noticed how quiet people seem to dislike loud people and vice versa? Matching the other person's vocal volume is a great way to gain quick rapport, to which I can definitely testify. Most people go quiet if they come into contact with a loud boss or authority figure. This is the **opposite** of what you should do. This can be seen as a sign of weakness by the person concerned and nothing that you say will have any bearing after that. What you should do is match that person's volume and tonality, as this conveys "He/she is on my wavelength". Do not be afraid to use this, as this could be your greatest asset for getting a promotion. It works for relationships too. For instance, when I was first studying my craft I was still living at home. I used to practise my new rapport skills all the time to see if I could influence my family (sorry, family!). Whenever my mother was in a bad mood, instead of tiptoeing around her as I had done previously, I would match her mood and adopt the same voice tone and mannerisms as her and I found that I could get her to change her mood by "**pacing and leading**" her. This technique is where you help to change a person's state from negative to positive by matching the other person's physiology for a few minutes and establishing rapport. Once rapport is established, you can begin to move the person away from his or her current state by changing your posture, breathing and tonality, and wait for them to follow. If they change with you, then you have successfully paced and then led them. This way you are more able to influence them or put forward your ideas without the usual barriers or resistance. Please note that this should be used only for the good of the person involved and for ethical reasons only.

The final piece of the piece of the rapport jigsaw is the **body language** aspect. The physical mirroring of a person by posture and breathing is an important part of gaining that trust and bond with a person. Whenever you see two people in love or two best friends talking next time you're out, notice the positioning of those people. Quite often their body language is like a reflection and their physical positioning of their bodies is the same. The same can be said of people who have no rapport, where their bodies and physiology are opposite to each other's. He might have his arms crossed and she might have her legs crossed away from him, indicating a break in rapport. The unconscious signal to the other person with whom you wish to gain rapport is that of **trust** when you mirror the physiology of that person. It's picked up unconsciously and the message you are sending is "I am like you, so you like me". It is very important to understand, though, that there is a big distinction between mirroring somebody and mimicking somebody. If you mimic somebody you will certainly upset him or her, so you have to be subtle with your mirroring so as not to cause offence. If a person has their legs crossed towards you, do the same and see what happens. Begin to match their physiology and tonality but don't be obvious about it. At first this can seem like a lot to remember but with practice it will become second nature. This knowledge and understanding might just help to make your life a little easier.

What could this knowledge be useful for?

- **Influencing your boss**
- **Negotiating a pay rise**
- **Gaining empathy with a friend**
- **Getting a table in a busy restaurant**
- **Understanding people**
- **Building friendships**
- **Strengthening your marriage**
- **Job interviews**
- **Negotiating deals**
- **Getting what you want.**

Let it go!

How many times do we encounter things that we get angry about? Quite a lot, no doubt, but how many times do we drag it out and make it into a bigger thing than it really was? Why do we do this; what do we get out of it? The answer is: not a lot. All we do is mentally punish ourselves by reliving the scenario over and over in our heads. If an incident occurs that doesn't really affect our lives or our families then we should **let it go**. If it doesn't really affect us as a person, other than by annoying us for a while, then let it go. If the result will be that we **will** be letting it go, we might as well let it go straight away rather than later. However, some people feel the need mentally to record every annoying event that happens in their day, to replay it to their loved ones later when they get home. They sit there all day, mentally replaying the event in their heads, over and over, again getting more and more steamed up about it (remember that your thoughts control your feelings). So when their poor unsuspecting partner comes through the door they are greeted with the "bad news" straight away. This sets the night up on a negative theme straightaway, which leads to a bad night's company. While the person rants and raves about the injustice of the incident their partner looks vacant and thinks to themselves "It's no big deal". This "lack of understanding" then leads to a row, as all that the partner wanted to do was wind down from work when they got home. If this is repeated on a daily basis the partner soon becomes sick of it and starts to avoid the " daily drama" and starts staying out late to escape. Like the story about the boy who cried wolf, after a while the stories become dull and predictable when the person's imagined worst case scenario doesn't happen again. When this happens any **real** drama is never believed any more.

If something doesn't really affect you or the world as a whole, other than annoying you a bit, just let it go!

When I talk to people it never fails to amaze me how wound up they get over the silliest little things — things that if you were to let them go would never matter. The other day I was speaking with a guy who'd recently come back from a holiday in Portugal. He told me in very specific detail about how angry he was to find an English waiter serving in the Portuguese restaurant where he went for a meal. He fumed "I didn't go all the way to Portugal from England to be served by an English waiter!". He was steaming at this point as he told me about another restaurant where he went to for a traditional English Sunday roast (in Portugal!), which didn't have the same style of Yorkshire puddings as he gets at home. To this guy it was a big deal but those people who could overhear the conversation must have thought he was an idiot. It was almost as if he thought the whole of Portugal should have known in advance of his exact requirements! I tried to point out to him that he was in fact in a foreign country and that allowances have to be made for the difference in culture but I was wasting my breath. The amazing part, though, is that people have the ability to recreate exactly the **same feelings** when telling their story as if it happened an hour before, even though it happened weeks ago. I've seen people literally spitting with anger as they recount stories which are really no big deal. They make a big deal over nothing and remain angry about it by constantly rethinking about them. I recently came back from a holiday in Corfu, having stayed in an all-inclusive hotel. The hotel was pretty average and the food was O.K. but not out of this world. However, the price that we paid to stay there was reasonable so we got what we paid for. We made the best of the holiday, hired a car and toured the island and ended up having a good time. Some guests, though, decided to stay in the hotel all night and day and those people soon found plenty to criticise. Whenever a new batch of holiday-makers turned up with their cases these people would immediately inform them that the hotel was no good and that they wouldn't enjoy their stay. I came into the bar one evening to find a guy sitting looking glum. When I asked what was wrong he told me that he'd just arrived and before he'd put his cases down the others had told him about all that was wrong with the hotel. This guy had saved up all year to take his family to this resort and now he wished he hadn't bothered. I told him to forget about those doom and gloom merchants and to make the best of his holiday as we had.

Every time we get angry our bodies release adrenalin into our bloodstream, attacking our bodily organs, so:

Don't feel the need to tell everybody about every negative thing that happened in your day.

You don't have to relive it again and again and infect them either. Some people can't wait to "get off their chest" their bad news to any poor soul who happens to have the misfortune of knowing them. You know the type: five minutes after bumping into them you feel like choking yourself as the once happy day turns into a gloomy one. These types are like an infection in that if you give them your valuable time they will leave you feeling ill. To these prophets of doom their job is to tell everybody how bad the world really is. Have you ever had the experience of having a friend phone you and get all worked up over something that you thought was no big deal? Usually afterwards you felt drained and wished they hadn't called. The next time they ring you pretend that you're not in! This is not being an uncaring friend because it doesn't help them if you sympathise every time something trivial occurs of which they exaggerate. Sympathising in situations like this is actually doing your friend **more harm** because if you do you are teaching them to be weak. This weak personality trait is the hallmark of the conscious mind thinker; if you really want to help them, tell them to buy this book!

If the world doesn't need to hear it, DON'T SAY IT!

Nowadays whenever I go anywhere I am not known, I don't tell people that I am a therapist. If I do, I get swarmed by people dying to tell me about their "problems". Often their problems are so trivial that if they let them go they could move on quickly. I used to know a man who never had anything positive to say. He would moan about everything: kids, buses, planes, trains, dogs, cats and anything else he could be "disappointed" by. He would literally drain the life out of you: if you gave him ten minutes, he could convince you that the world that you were seeing was false and that it really was a negative, horrible place. He died of cancer in his early fifties. I never heard one person who knew him say one good thing about him when he died. Normally people are able to think about one good thing to say about somebody but the overall opinion was that he wouldn't be missed. The funniest thing happened before he died though; he became a nice man. It took terminal cancer to make him appreciate how special life was.

Why is it that whenever people survive an ordeal — whether it is cancer, a plane crash or something similar — they have a greater appreciation of life? Suddenly they notice the birds in the trees, the beautiful sunset or the smell of a rose as they come to realise how precious life is and how much a gift our being human is. When they realise they are losing it, it is as if everything is put in perspective. I believe that we are truly privileged to be where we are and should live every day as if it were our last. You don't have to go through a traumatic ordeal in order to appreciate your life; you can do it now. Stop moaning about how life is so much better for other (lucky) people and not you and remember those people who are less fortunate than ourselves; they'd love to live like we do. If we only have one life on this earth —and, as far as we know, we do — **let's make the best of it RIGHT NOW and start living it!**

Chapter Six

Principle 6: Create the Life You Want

Is this important? You bet it's important! I know of no successful person who has ever lived on this planet who didn't know what he or she wanted to achieve beforehand. The easiest and most powerful way to begin to do this is by writing down your plan in the form of a mission statement. The subject of goal-setting via a mission statement is not a new concept or even an original idea, but I don't think I have ever read any personal development material that hasn't covered this subject, even if only for a little bit. Here's why: if you lived in the UK and you wanted to drive overseas to Germany for the first time would you just set off and hope to get there on time without any planning? Or would you need some sort of a map to make sure you didn't get lost? Of course you would need a map otherwise you could end up anywhere and you'd probably take many wrong turns along the way. This is what most people do though when they don't have any plans for their life. They set off without planning how they are going to arrive at their chosen destination if they even have one. Remember you won't get to Germany if you don't first have a map!

When you design the life that you want, you go from being a passive witness to the creator, designer and owner of your life.

Isn't this just goal-setting?

What I want to do now is to broach this important topic with a different outlook. Whenever I give my clients a printout of the Principles of Life, the following week I ask them if they have finished their mission statement. To that they usually reply: "I haven't had the time" or "I forgot". I would say that 95 per cent of all my clients who take the Principles of Life home with them never take the time to write down their mission statement. Why, though? Why don't people take ten minutes to sit down and really think about what they want to be in life or what they would really like to achieve? The answer is **fear!**

It is the fear of not being able to live up to the standard that you set for yourself in your mission statement. What following a mission statement also means is that you are no longer able to act like an asshole in life any more, and that can be a scary thought. It means that once you have the statement written down you no longer have any excuses for being lazy and moaning about life. It means taking the ultimate responsibility for yourself, and that can be a little daunting. It can be the reason that so many people put off doing it because then you **have** to do it otherwise you are breaking a commitment to yourself. All the time I see people pretending to be blasé about the whole thing when they are really frightened of making that kind of commitment. Self-doubt is a big factor in whether such a statement is ever made.

Let's have a look at your life. How are things going? Is your life everything that you wanted it to be? If not, why not? How's your working life? Are you fulfilled in what you are doing or is it not working out for you in the way that you wanted? If what you're doing in life is not working out for you, maybe it isn't **meant** to be working out for you. Maybe you're not doing the things that you **should** be doing. Maybe it's not your **plan** to be doing what you're doing now and maybe the feelings that you have about your life are the signals that are telling you that you should be taking a different course. Let me ask you some questions: Are you struggling in your life? Are you being all that you could be? Do you think that the person that you are today is the person that you're here to be? Is this what you're here for? I understand that these are pretty big questions, which can seem a little "spiritual" to some people, but they don't have to be part of any religion. You see, I find that people who do not have a path in life never live a truly satisfied life; they just amble through it. The worst part about that is that all those people could have been so much more. Please don't be afraid. I know these questions open up a whole can of worms but maybe the can **had** to open up and that's why you somehow bought this book. So don't worry about asking yourself these questions. Maybe it's time to get on the right path or maybe you are already on it.

"The scariest thing is to not know your place in this world ...to not know why you are here ... it's an awful feeling."
Samuel L. Jackson in Unbreakable

It's time to confront your doubts and fears and really begin to take the knowledge from this book so that it's put to its proper use.

Let me ask you some more questions. Please write down the answers in the spaces provided. Do not worry about writing in this book, it is your book so if somebody else wants to read it they will have to buy a copy for themselves just like you did. Go on get a pen!

Regardless of whether you think it is possible or not, what would you REALLY like to do in your life?

...

...

...

...

What's preventing you from doing it?

...

...

...

...

What are your strengths?

...

...

...

...

What would you like to be better at?

...

...

Who are your heroes or heroines?

...

...

Do you think you are everything you could be?.............If not, what stops you?

...

...

...

Do you think that success and happiness are things that happen only to "lucky" people?.........
Does change scare you?..............

Or does it excite you?............
Do you procrastinate?..........
Can people become more intelligent with age?.........
Do you have limiting beliefs about yourself?............If so, what are they?...
..
What beliefs do you have about yourself that are empowering?
..
..
..
...
Do you believe in God or a higher being?
..
Do you believe your life has a purpose? ....
Why?..
..
..
..

These questions should get your wise mind thinking about yourself and your life generally. You may be surprised at your answers.

I don't know what to do!

Many people who come to see me tell me that they are not happy in their jobs. They tell me that they are unfulfilled and cannot imagine doing the same job for the rest of their lives. When I ask them what job would they like to do instead they usually say "I don't know".

To that I always say: "What would be your dream job"? The answer to **that** question is the job that they **should** be doing, and that goes for **you** too! Whatever your dream job would be is the job you should be doing (regardless of whether you think you could do it or not). If you single-mindedly apply yourself to do whatever it takes to achieve your dream job, you will get there in the end. Remember that somebody had the same dream as you and they are now doing now what **you** want to do!

To be truly fulfilled, you must be doing your dream job. Anything less and you won't ever be satisfied.

Why bother writing a mission statement?

That's a good question: why should we bother? If you want to live a mediocre life and you are not bothered whether you succeed in life or not, then don't bother. If you prefer to moan that life is hard and that you never get the "lucky breaks" that other people get, then don't bother either. But if you want to live the best life that you can, you **must** have some goals. The mission statement is the easiest and quickest way to achieve your goals. It's the road map that tells you where you need to go.
The beauty of doing this is that you will achieve them in **half the time or less**, whereas if you had just **thought** about your goals they might never happen at all. As long as the goals are realistically achievable within the time frame that you give them, you will find that they can be achieved. This does not mean, however, that if you don't do anything to actually make them happen they will still be achieved — not at all. What it does mean is that now that you have a plan of what you need to do you can concentrate on the job in hand. It is sensible to set down one or two **main** goals for the year, with maybe some **minor** or less important ones to follow if you still have the time to spare. The main goals should be very important to you and be ones which, when actualised, will totally change your life. The reason I say that you should have only one or two main goals is because when you have too many written down it can then become too daunting when you look at them and you may give up. I've seen people who had written 20 goals for the year, with some of them very difficult to achieve, become disillusioned after a month and give up. On the other hand, what usually happens when you write down just a couple is that because there is less to concentrate on, you will achieve the goals in no time and then you could be ready to start on some more! This builds self-confidence, whereas giving up after a month because of overdoing it takes self-confidence away.

Let me give you an example. This year I wrote down two main goals that I really wanted to achieve. The first one was that I was going to write this book and because of my busy lifestyle I was going to give myself a year to do it. The second one was that I was going to put some muscle on my frame and get my body weight from 180 pounds to 210 pounds within the year too. Here's what happened. Because I had only these two main goals I found that I became driven to achieve them as never before. The result was that I finished the book in five months (seven months early) and upped my body weight to 210 pounds in seven months with weight training. Because I had achieved these goals much more quickly than even I had expected, I now had time to concentrate on my minor goals. This has to be tried for yourself for you to really see what I'm talking about. You can make your goals a part of your mission statement or you can write them down separately — it's up to you. Remember that your mission statement is your long-term goal plan.

I've seen study after study on goal-setting and its effects on people's lives; and the mountain of evidence is that goal-setting is necessary to ensure success is incontrovertible. I could go on and on, quoting different testimonials to substantiate this but, frankly, I can't be bothered. This has been done so many times in lots of previous books and I'm concerned with giving you only quality information. This is because, even if you do write down a mission statement, if you haven't got the right attitude then it will never be actualised. The fact is this: most of the world's population does not succeed beyond the level of the average, the reason being that they don't have any real goals to work towards. Or the ones they do have aren't ambitious enough to really yield anything out of this world. If that's what you want, then that's O.K. but, let's face it, if you didn't really want to improve some or even all of the aspects of your life, then you wouldn't have bought a personal development book, would you? Let's **get real**: you want to be better, think smarter and have an even more fulfilling life, don't you? People who say that they are happy with mediocrity are really trying to convince themselves that they are. Actually, they fear change, even if they beg to differ. People get stuck in their comfort zones because they listen to their conscious minds too much.

Visualise this. Imagine that life is a highway with five lanes. The highway is nose to tail with cars all moving forwards. The first four lanes from left to right are the "ordinary Joe" lanes, where everybody is bumper to bumper and travelling at the same pace. Nothing much happens in this lane as there is nowhere to go but steadily onwards. Everybody just follows the person ahead because to change course would upset the apple cart. In these lanes the outcome is predictable and although the people would love to change direction, they don't know how or don't think that they can. With this belief in mind they just follow the course, hoping that it will change via some miracle.

The last lane on the right, though, looks different. This is the "mission" lane, where everybody knows where they want to go. These cars are going much faster and there are many slip roads to come off on. Every now and then, a car takes one of these turns down a slip road and a new direction is taken. These drivers have the proper maps in front of them and they know which direction they need to take in order for them to reach the place where they want to be. These drivers enjoy the variety of having many choices and the benefit of choosing their destination, rather than "seeing where we end up". Which lane do you want to be in?

This simple metaphor shows how the different lanes bring very different outcomes. Most people live in the left lanes and leave things to fate or hope. Every now and then, one will get lucky but the majority will not. The right lane ,though, are the goal-setters; these people know what they want and they are determined to get it. Not every goal-setter becomes a super-achiever or a millionaire; this is because not every goal-setter wants this. Some just want to help others or do some good in the world, both of which are excellent goals to have. Goals are the key to getting what you want.

Without some goals you are leaving it up to fate, which always yields mediocre outcomes.

I'm going to make some assumptions. I think you want a better life; I think you want to have greater peace of mind; and I also think you want to be successful in some endeavour or another. Whether that is in your family life, your relationships or your professional field, I believe that you bought this book to help you do just that. I have read many books, that have provided me with scraps of quality information, which in time have helped me to mould this information into knowledge. That knowledge is what I share with you here. You must trust this knowledge and **apply** it straight away if you want your life to be better than average. So let's cut to the chase.

Mission statement

To most people, the thought of writing a mission statement is a little daunting. This is because most people have the false idea that it requires a lot of writing. In fact, the amount of writing is not as important as the amount of thought required. A simple company mission statement could be "Always to value the customer"; a personal mission statement could be as simple as "I'm going to live the best life ever and be as successful as I can". This is just an example of a simple but empowering mission statement, which is the **core** of your goals. If you said "I want to be a millionaire and have a Ferrari and live in a big house with acres of land", yes, these are goals but they do not form a mission statement. The mission statement asks the question "why do you want those things?". The answer to that question should be the core of the mission statement. These things may be things that add up to or contribute to your mission statement but they are **not** the mission statement. The mission statement is the centre of your world, the driving force that decides what decisions you take in life. It is the pivot upon which you assess all major decisions or directions that you take. This does not mean that a mission statement cannot change, because quite often on our journey to personal happiness we encounter new experiences that can alter the way forward for us. As long as the mission statement has the same integrity as it had when it was first conceived, it's O.K. to change it along the way. For instance, you may have been single at the time of writing it and may now need to include some new people in there!

So what is there to think about when you write a mission statement?

First of all, what you need to think seriously about is what you want for your life. What is it that you want to achieve and why? What would you **really** like to do in your life? Who would you like to be? Do not think that you have to restrict yourself at this point; you can put down whatever you want. The only limits that you have are the ones that you believe you have. **Who do you REALLY want to be?**

Don't get bogged down with whether you think this is possible or not yet, because with more practice and determination you will be able to transform yourself into whatever you want. This is the point of this book: to help you become the person that deep down inside you really are. Once we get rid of the old garbage that holds you back, the real you will be set free. Think about it: you have been holding yourself back, haven't you? Your own self-doubts have stopped you so many times and you could kick yourself sometimes because you let the fear of failure stop you. It's O.K., we have all done this, but now it's time to find your courage, the courage that says "I am not afraid any more — my life starts now!", and to begin to take charge of your life.

Let's start by defining who you really are, what you stand for and what kind of person you're committed to being.

Please write down the answers in the spaces provided below.

Who am I?...
....
....
What do I believe in?...
....
....
What moves or inspires me?...
....
....
What do I want from my life?..
....
....
....
Who do I love? Why?...
....
....
What am I here to do?..
....
....
....

You did fill out the answers, didn't you? Because if you didn't, I'm going to come round to your house and make you do them! Please do them. The answers to these questions should start the ball rolling and get you thinking about your life and who you really are, what you stand for and what is important to you. These things **must** be taken into consideration when you begin to make your mission statement.

"If one does not know to which port one is sailing, no wind is favourable."
Seneca

What is your true purpose in this world anyway?

Boy, is that a **big** question; it's a King Kong of a question! First, let me explain what it doesn't mean. It doesn't mean that I think you are here to save the world or to be the next Mother Teresa or Ghandi. But what I want you to think about when I ask that question is "Do you think that you are here to be the person that you are right now?". If, for instance, you have a weight problem that you have been battling for years, do you think you are here to be the person who has a life-long weight problem? Or do you think there might be another reason or plan for you that may not be in play because most of your life is taken up with your daily weight battle? If you suffer from depression, do you think that you're here to be just another depressive person in the world, or do you think there is more to you than that? Is there another person inside who is screaming to get out? Come on, now is the time to say "Enough is enough"; it's time to be who you **really are** and who you were meant to be. It's time to free yourself from the shackles and start living your life the way you were supposed to be living it! By the way, this is not a religious question; it applies to all people regardless of what you believe in. Even if you do not believe in God, the same applies. We have to start taking charge of our lives, and having goals is the key.

How do you want to be remembered when you're gone?

If you had the opportunity of watching your own funeral, what would you want people to say about you? This may seem a strange question but think about it: if you were sitting at the back of the church or mosque watching the proceedings and one by one people came to the front to speak about you, what would you like them to say? Imagine that somebody you worked with stood up and talked about you: what would you like him or her to say? What would you think they would say now? If a friend stood up and spoke, what would you like them to say about you? If a family member stood up and spoke, what would you like them to say about you? The chances are that you wouldn't want them to stand and say "She was a real drag to work with" or "He was always moaning about his life; he's much better off now!" or even "My Mum was so depressed and moody that it's a relief now for all of us that she's gone". Of course not — what you would want them to say is that you were a great person, a true friend or the best partner they could ever have wanted.

When you leave this earth, leave your mark. Make an impression, no matter how small, as long as it's a positive one for the world as a whole.

Some time ago I remember watching a documentary about the late actor Michael Landon. For those who don't know who he was, he was the star of the *Little House on the Prairie* and *Highway to Heaven* T.V. series. I was so moved to hear the testimonials from people who had known him that the documentary had a profound effect on me. Every person had a story to tell about how he had touched their lives in a positive way and that he had been a powerful, positive inspiration to those who knew him. Some of the stories were brilliant and he will be so badly missed by those who loved him. It got me thinking about my own life and I wondered what people would say about me if I were to die suddenly. From then on, I wanted to be remembered in the same way so I decided to live the sort of life where I would be a positive influence on any person I met. I still strive to do that. Bear these things in mind when you write your mission statement on the next page. Well, what are you waiting for? I've already got you started!

Mission Statement

"……………………………………………………………………………

……………………………………………………………………………

……………………………………………………………………………"

This mission statement gives me the framework so that every decision I make will either take me towards my mission statement or away from it.

In order to reach this position and maintain it there are some specific things I must do or be. These are:

I am committed to this mission statement and will do my very best to make this a reality in my life for the good of myself and for the world as a whole.

Signed……………………………………………………Dated………

"The purpose of life is a life of purpose."
Buddha

Please do not proceed any further unless you have written your mission statement. Now that you have your mission statement written out, it's time to:

Begin to put it into practice!

That's right, now that you have your goals in front of you, what you need to do is to start to live by them. Whatever you wrote, there will definitely be some steps you have to take in order for you to reach them. Along the way there will be obstacles, some physical and some mental. What we are going to do here is begin to show you how we can eliminate those barriers by adopting a new mental attitude. The first new mental attitude is:

1. Think of all obstacles as CHALLENGES

The way of the confident, proactive individual is never to see things as obstacles or problems; instead they view them as challenges. "Yeah, there are a few **challenges** but I'll soon sort them out" is a typical statement from someone of this mindset. Begin to change this wording into **your** vocabulary and things will start to sort themselves out. It's also more challenging to have a challenge than to have a problem. Begin to switch the words "problems", "nightmares", "obstacles", and "difficulties" into the word "challenges". Once you do this, you will see why I ask you to do it, because it works like magic. Problems disappear!

2. Think of problems as challenges to conquer

When we think of the problems that occur in our daily lives as challenges instead, it gives us a different perspective to think about. Most of us like challenges more than we like problems so by simply changing the wording it can even give us a buzz at the thought of solving the problem rather than being anxious.

When we think of difficulties as problems they begin to drain us mentally and we start to feel like we're fighting an uphill battle. When we think of difficulties as challenges, though, it's as if a gauntlet has been thrown down for us to take up. It then becomes a battle of us versus the challenge! I like solving challenges more than I like dealing with problems. The magical thing that happens when we use this new perspective is that we feel eager to solve the challenges. We rarely warm to the idea of dealing with problems in the same way. When we begin to think of difficulties as challenges rather than problems we actually want to solve them. Also, it is more fun to think about a challenge that we have to deal with, which we can get excited about solving.

Even personal problems like making a marriage work can be thought of as a challenge where the challenge could be to fix it in the fastest time by doing whatever it takes. Or if there's somebody at work that you find it impossible to get on with, you could use this as a challenge to see if your rapport skills can help to change the situation. You could have some real fun with this by trying different techniques that you have learned from the section on rapport. If you smoke, you could make stopping a challenge for yourself.

We can make our challenges as easy or hard as we want just by attaching our thoughts to them. Think they are hard and they will be so; think they are easy and they will be also.

The challenge in this case could be not only to stop smoking but also to do it with a big smile on your face at the same time. This would shock a lot of people! The challenge could be to do it differently from everybody else who has tried in your office and who craved and became grouchy. You could **decide** that your challenge is to do it with the happiest and funniest behaviour that people could expect. You can make change fun as it's always your choice. The possibilities are endless with this new mindset. Why not behave in the **opposite** way of other people faced with the same difficulty? You could have fun with that one. It's just a question of making a decision to do it; at first it might seem silly or even impossible to do, but think about it. Who says that we have to react or behave in the ways that do? We only do so because we have learned to do so by watching other people.

Have you ever wondered how you learned to react in the ways that you do? The answer is simple; we learned by watching other people and practising until it became second nature. We don't have to act or react in **any** of the old ways, though, just by **deciding** to have a different reaction next time a situation arises where you previously behaved in a certain way. If you usually get angry when you hit traffic jams you could decide to react totally differently the next time; maybe smile and shout "Hallelujah, I love traffic!" or something equally as outrageous. You could think "What is the opposite of my old behaviour?" and do that instead. Why not? You'll probably laugh out loud as you try this and you might decide to stick with it.

If you have some negative character traits or unwanted behaviours, try this. Think "What is the opposite of my current behaviour?" and imagine yourself doing that. It may look funny, imagining doing it this way, but why not actually give it a go? What have you got to lose? You're not happy with the old way, so things can only get better, can't they? Make these things the new challenges to put into practice rather than viewing them as problems.

Look forward to new challenges

That's right, actually look forward to them! Most people shy away from new challenges, often because their own negative thinking puts them off. This mindset must be installed into your mind if the mission statement is ever going to materialise. It is also the mindset of the world's most successful people so you can be sure that it is 100 per cent spot on. We need challenge in our lives otherwise they become dull and predictable.

"Life is either a daring adventure or nothing."
Helen Keller: American blind/deaf author and lecturer

Let's take the example of two friends, Walter and Peter, two men of equal intelligence who had obtained the same degree in business studies with exactly the same grades. Walter didn't believe in writing down goals because he wanted to see where life would take him. Walter got a job in a local university as a business lecturer and earned a modest wage. Peter, on the other hand, had studied the strategies of most successful business people of the world and found that the common denominator was that they all had a clear vision of who and where they wanted to be in life. Peter wrote down the goals that he wanted for his life and referred to them every day. Peter started his own business and pretty soon began to make big money, which was one of his goals. Walter pretty much stayed the same, with a wage increase every year in line with inflation. He hoped his "luck" would change one day but the years went by without much change. He told himself that his unfulfilled potential was because of the economic climate and that he was wise to stay in his "safe" job. Meanwhile, Peter expanded his businesses and become a part-time consultant, working whenever he felt like it as the income from his other businesses kept him in his millionaire lifestyle, which was also one of his goals. A few years later Walter bumped into Peter in a smart restaurant and they chatted about their university days. Walter was surprised when he found out that the smart restaurant they met in was one of many that Peter owned. When Walter asked Peter how come he had been so "lucky", Peter laughed and explained that it was down not to luck but to having his goals set up in his early life, which guided him to make the right decisions. Walter told Peter he didn't believe in goal-setting. After they finished chatting, they both left, Walter in his Lada and Peter in his Mercedes.

Setting YOUR Goals in YOUR Mind

When you know what you want with your goals, you have to be sure you'll be happy when you achieve them!

1. **Close your eyes and relax.**
2. **Get a clear picture in your mind of what you really desire.**
3. **See it as if you already have it. Imagine yourself in the scene, enjoying whatever it is.**
4. **Hear all the sounds around you and let what you're hearing reverberate around as you immerse yourself into this scene.**
5. **Really begin to see and feel what it feels like to have achieved your goal. Enjoy it!**

Remember: Your mind is a goal-oriented machine and what ever you focus your mind on, your mind will help you to achieve it.

Start to become curious about life

Life has so many things to offer us: different places to see, different things to learn. There is a whole new world open up to us right now that wasn't there before. There are opportunities out there staring us in the face, waiting for us to collect when we start to look for them. Once we start looking for them, they begin to stand out. Recently I became interested in learning how to trade on the world's stock markets. As soon as I got interested in it, I become astonished at how many opportunities to learn about it I came across. I opened up a newspaper and found a whole bunch of free information about stocks and shares, which I never noticed before because I wasn't looking for it. A couple of days later I was talking to a friend and I mentioned my interest, whereupon I was shown a course that would help me get started. Now every time I pick up the newspaper these things just pop out at me. They were there all the time but, before, I wasn't looking. You see, there are opportunities there all the time but if you don't look for them they drift away and somebody else takes them. So start to build up your curiosity for life. What could you do to really interest yourself? What exciting things could you be doing that you would never dream of doing before? Get curious about them, and get curious about life!

Never "Try" to do something

If two guys were at the bottom of a mountain and one says "I am going to **try** and climb that mountain" and the other guy says "I am going to climb that mountain". Which one would you put your money on to do it? The one who's going to **try**, or the one who is **going to do it**. This may seem trivial but it is not. When we try to do something it means that you have an expectation that you will fail. Never try to do anything. Either do it or don't. Don't give yourself a get out clause with the word try. If a client tells me they will try something I say "Don't bother trying either do it or don't".

Enjoy learning about yourself!

Whenever we start to think about doing new things we must accept that when we start, we are not going to be perfect. One of the most pleasurable things that I have learned as I mature is to enjoy learning about myself. I never fail to be amazed by just how easy trying new things is when you use this philosophy. Ask yourself "How good can I be?" whenever you undertake something new. How good could you be at X or Y? If you have an idea that you would like to pursue, start to ask yourself that very question. How far can you take yourself? How far can you take this new goal? Let your imagination go wild!

We have a free rein over our minds and how we choose to use them. We don't have to go the prescribed way just because everybody else is going that way.

Delete the words "can't" and "but what if" from your vocabulary

These words are two of the biggest killers of any kind of ambition and personal growth there are. Using these words in our vocabulary kills off any chance of living our lives to their true potential. These extremely common words are used extensively by the conscious mind thinker and can cause much misery and self-doubt. The person who uses these words in their thoughts and in their general vocabulary is a person who is going to be very limited indeed. You must delete those words from your mind and your vocabulary if a successful life is what you desire. These are the words used universally by the loser and failure in life. If you want to be a winner and a success you must understand the power of those negative words in their ability to sabotage any chance of living a fantastic life. First of all let's deal with the word "**can't**".

The most important thing that you need to know about the word "can't" is that, except in cases of impossibility, it really means "won't". When I first went to college to study psychotherapy, my teacher informed me that the first thing I had to do for my homework was to delete the word "can't" from my vocabulary. To that I said "But I can't!". With this in mind, I reluctantly agreed that he was right and that "can't" really did mean "won't", so I mentally started to delete it from my vocabulary. It was quite difficult at first because in the past I would use it quite often when something came up that I didn't want to do. It was so easy just to say "I can't" and then avoid doing something; it was my escape clause whenever I didn't really want to do something. But I was keen and disciplined and I decided that not saying "can't" had to be done if I really wanted to grow up and start to take full responsibility for myself. I would catch myself out all the time and I was shocked at how many times I would use the word throughout the day. I would painfully change the end of the sentence where previously I would have said "can't" in mid-speech. With the words of my teacher echoing in my mind — "'can't' means 'won't'" — I finally changed for good. It was one of the best pieces of advice I have ever taken and this is why I offer it to you. Since I took that advice and deleted the word "can't" I have found that there isn't anything I really can't do and I find myself doing things now that I used to think were impossible. **You** can too!

Does "can't" always mean "won't"?

Total impossibility is the only exception to the rule. If you were to say "I can't fly out of my bedroom window", I would agree. But if you said to me "I can't stand up in public and make a speech", well this is a **won't** situation. When you say "I can't" to yourself what you are really saying is that it is impossible. In the case of the first example I would agree that at this present time that it is impossible to fly unaided, but the second example, of speaking in public, is definitely not impossible; if it were true, the world would not be full of successful public speakers. Public speaking takes both knowledge and practice to perfect but it is certainly not impossible. It is also not possible solely for charismatic people. Anybody can become a good speaker with practice and the correct knowledge of the subject which is to be spoken about. As I say to my clients:

"Just chop the T off the end of can't, and you will find things much easier."

Next let's deal with the words "**but what if**".

This little phrase is the phrase of choice for the conscious mind thinker. This phrase is a dead giveaway for telling me if the person is conscious mind-driven or not. It is used extensively when a person has an over-active conscious mind and is usually accompanied by some kind of negative paranoid statement. Something negative **always** comes after using those words, as in these examples:

"But what if I can't do it?"
"But what if they don't like me?"
"But what if I can't get there on time?"
"But what if I can't do the work?"
"But what if I fail?"

After such a statement is made, the conscious mind thinker then runs through negative scenarios, seeing themselves in a very negative predicament. They believe this is acting as a "safeguard" which helps them when doing something which is perceived to be risky or scary (which the conscious mind makes up). Often totally ridiculous scenarios run through our minds like mini movies, which act as "proof" in order to back up this way of thinking. These movies then become believed and the person avoids the situation at all costs. Take the example of Ben. Ben was asked to be best man at his friend's wedding but two weeks before the big day he begins to have some doubts. He'd really like to do it, "But what if I begin to stutter when I get up there?", he thinks, and "But what if nobody laughs at my jokes and I just die up there?" Then he mentally reviews a mini movie imagining those scenarios with horrible endings. Suddenly his stomach is in knots and he really begins to have serious doubts over the challenge. During the lead-up to the wedding he reviews the negative scenarios in his head every day, over and over, until on the day of the wedding he won't go through with it. He imagines the outcome to be so dramatically bad that he physically cannot stand up.

Take too the example of Barbara. Barbara was astonished to hear one day that her conscientious work and diligence had not gone unnoticed in the office and a promotion had come up. Barbara was elated and was looking forward to the trip to London for the interview, which was more of a formality than a test. Three days later the gremlins had got into her mind and had started to do their evil work as the "but what ifs" started. She thought "But what if I get there and I get lost in the big city?" and "But what if I get mugged in the underground or get the wrong train?" and "But what if I freeze in the interview and make a fool of myself?", and so on. With these thoughts firmly in her mind, she now felt terrified at the prospect of going to London and declined the promotion. These examples are typical things that I hear from clients every week whenever they come to see me with challenges such as irrational fears. These fears are brought about by nothing more than the negative thinking of the "but what if" syndrome.

When you delete the words "can't" and "but what if" from your vocabulary, something magical happens. You will find that you can!

There IS a cure!

Whenever people come into my office with such stories of woe, I tell them to change the words from "but what if" to "so what if". "So what if it doesn't work?" "So what if people don't like me?" "So what if I don't get the job? As long as I tried my utmost, then that is all I can do." This is the same philosophy I have with the clients I work with. It is inevitable that every now and then, for some reason, no matter what I say or do, it doesn't work for them. In the past this used to be a constant source of inner conflict for me but now I think more clearly and wisely about it. I have accepted that I am not God and that there will be times when, for whatever reason, therapy will not yield any change with a client, and I am at peace with that now. It may be that the client needs to take a different course of treatment or avenue, and that this therapy wasn't meant to work. It's got nothing to do with myself or the client doing something wrong; it is simply that it cannot work for every single person on the planet, otherwise I would be perfect, and I'm not! As long as we do our very best, then it is O.K. if things don't always succeed, and that goes for exams, interviews, speaking in public or anything that requires effort. You must have the same mindset in your life that as long as you did your very best then that is all you can do. The key for personal growth through this is yet again achieved by asking yourself the question "What can I learn from this?" when things don't work out the way you wanted them to.

With this mindset you are onto a winner; you cannot lose unless you want to.

Chapter Seven

Principle 7: Stop Letting Your Mind Poison You!

This is an important chapter and principle to follow. If you don't, you're going to run into problems. A lot of people have their minds run them instead of them running their minds. All the time I see people who are victims of their own thinking and because of that they go through life as if it were one big battle. You must begin to take charge of your mind because if you don't, things can get pretty scary. Your mind can be your best friend or your worst enemy, depending on how much control you have over it.

The little voice in your head can take you either away from your goals or towards them, depending on whether or not you allow it to dictate you. The little voice in your head is your conscious mind and we have already discussed how running your life by it can be disastrous. You must follow your wisdom; your wisdom is there but you have to listen for it. It doesn't appear as "in your face" as your conscious mind chatter does and you have to relax in order to receive it. It is the part of your mind that is behind your conscious mind chatter and when you bypass the conscious you gain access to the wise resources of your subconscious.

I see people both in my office and in the street who are tormented by their own minds. This lack of ability to really take charge of their thoughts is a constant thorn in their sides. We must stop being a passive force that becomes affected every time bad thoughts enter our heads. We must take charge. If we do not, we must suffer the consequences of our weakness and pay a heavy price. But it doesn't have to be this way; we can start to take the necessary steps to reverse the negative patterns of our thinking and start to live the lives we want. Is this really too much to ask? I don't think so, but what we have to remember is that to change this negative cycle is to fight the greatest battle there is. But it's worth it!

The first step to change is to stop letting that negative chatter belittle you. Tell it to shut up! You don't have to let every negative thing it says have a direct effect on you. If you let whatever it says run your life, then you're in for a rough time. For example, if your little voice tells you all the time that you are unattractive and you believe it, then you will mould you life around that thought. If it always tells you that you "can't" do things that you really can do and you go through life with that thought, then you would live a very limited life indeed. You need to know that you are the boss, so tell the little voice to shut up! Tell it that its opinion is bullshit! And, regardless of what **it** says to you, do not go by its opinion any more.

This might seem a little weird at first, but think about it: the little voice in your head is real and you can hear it all the time, can't you. People tend to let that voice overpower them when they really need to fight back. If you have a little voice that puts you off, why not develop an even bigger voice to spur you on? It's your head and your mind; why not begin to develop an even bigger voice that scares the little one away? The world's most successful people have the same little voice in their heads as we do but they have learned not to pay too much attention to it. Now whenever a sneaky negative thought pops into my mind, it runs scared as I have now developed an even bigger voice that cuts it down to size! You don't have to stand for it; you can take charge again. Here are some ideas to help change this process:

You must learn to run your mind or it will begin to run you!

The power of auto-suggestion

Tell yourself that you are **super-confident**. Even if you don't believe it, tell yourself that anyway because the more you say it, the more quickly it will come true. We become what we focus on and what we tell ourselves. If you want to be more confident then you must start to think this way and repeat that suggestion every day. This has got to be the oldest and most well used of all of the personal development techniques known. This form of repetition is known as auto-suggestion. There is nothing new about it; in fact, with the boom of personal development it was one of the first ways people used to help change themselves. So although it is hardly breakthrough technology that I am presenting here, it is nevertheless a very powerful change technique. There are lots of different ways to use auto-suggestion — let me show you a few.

The first one is simple and is one of the oldest techniques around; which is writing down what you want to be and reading it ten times, first thing every morning and last thing at night. Example: "I am super-confident and my confidence is increasing every day."

This may seem a little cheesy but it really works and is a great way to get the ball rolling in your personal development. I started using this when I was younger and it really worked; it helped me to start gaining the confidence that I now enjoy today. I never had somebody who would tell me something like that when I was a kid so after reading about the technique I began to apply it to myself. Rarely do we find parents who are great life coaches so sometimes we must take it upon ourselves to do it for ourselves.

The idea is that if you say the statement, or even just read it, first thing in the morning when you are still half-awake, this works in the same way as hypnosis and begins to program the mind. The mind is still coming out of the alpha brainwave state when we wake up, so it is **then** that we can start to program our minds with auto-suggestion. In the alpha state the mind is impressionable as it is the same brainwave state as is used in hypnosis. At that point you can either say out loud or read to yourself whatever positive affirmation you wish to have come true. This bypasses the usual critical faculty of the conscious mind and can be absorbed with less resistance. Just before bed is also a good time as, once again, the brainwaves are slowing down as you get ready for sleep. Twice a day should be sufficient and you should begin to feel some difference in a couple of weeks.

Next are some examples of positive affirmations that can be used or adapted for auto-suggestion. Remember that you don't have to believe these affirmations as you say or read them but think of them as your future outcomes:

- **My ability to store and recall information is increasing every day with practice. My memory is improving**
- **I am becoming more relaxed in all situations where I used to feel stressed or anxious. I am relaxing more every day.**
- **Every day my strength is improving and so is my ability to train harder. My body is becoming fitter and stronger every day.**
- **I am becoming more assertive every day and my opinion is not only worthwhile but also valuable.**
- **I am starting to appreciate my life more now and I now begin to see the positives from living this way.**
- **My life is getting better and every new day is an opportunity to live it to the full. Life is good.**
- **I am not a victim any more. I am a strong, powerful human being with a fresh outlook on life. I am not my past.**
- **I am a good golfer and every time I play, I learn a little more. This learning is making me a better golfer.**
- **I am learning to be less uptight, less angry, less stressed and less serious about life. Every day I am relaxing more.**
- **My belief in myself is increasing and so is my self-confidence. Every day I criticise myself less and love myself more.**
- **I now no longer pick faults with myself. It is pointless and dumb. I now accept and value myself.**

These are examples that you can either use or adapt for your own auto-suggestion. You could, if you wish, include some or all of the above affirmations on one piece of paper to recite or read first thing in the morning and last thing at night. It is important that you do it every day, though, as it needs repetition to make it a firm thought in your mind for it to really begin to start working.

It is better not to make any affirmations that are too unbelievable as this could cause a pressure build-up for yourself. Make them believable and achievable goals. Please don't write down "I am a stallion who can make love for hours and make any woman yell with pleasure" because you might be setting yourself (and your partner) up for disappointment!

We talk to ourselves everyday; why not talk to our selves to promote some good?

Another variation of auto-suggestion is when people ask us about ourselves. If you were to stop me in the street and ask me if I was a confident person I would immediately reply that I am "very confident". I have told myself that so many times that it is now a living fact! In the same way, if you were to ask me if I was happy I would always answer with a resounding "Yes". This goes for any personal question that you may ask me; I will always answer you with a positive. This is not self-delusion or living on Fantasy Island; every answer I give will be the truth. I have created the world that I live in and you can create yours. Responding positively to personal questions is a step towards their actualisation. Always answer in the positive because responding negatively will make both you and the person asking the question feel badly. Remember that we don't have to make a drama out of our lives. Whatever problems we have are **not forever** and they are not the sum total of our lives. We do have the power to change things by thinking wisely and making good choices and decisions about our lives.

What if I really do have a problem?

There is no problem, other than psychosis, that cannot be cured by using the many strategies in this book. Specify what it is and what you have to do in order to solve it and look up whatever exercise you may need to use to change it. Otherwise, if you need one-to-one help you can contact me or another healthcare professional who deals with the mind. You shouldn't need to, though; just look at the summary of exercises at the back of this book to show you where to find help if you get stuck. Remember that in almost all cases the cause is our **thinking**.

Audio auto-suggestion

This is a popular method that I have also used myself. It involves taking the affirmations you want to come true and recording them on to an audiocassette. You can record for as long as you like and read off a sheet of paper the affirmations you want for yourself, then listen to yourself speaking the affirmations instead. You could have your cassette player by your bed and wake up to them and go to sleep to them. This is really quite simple and for some people makes an easy job even easier. If you are living with someone, though, it would probably be better to use headphones because they might think you've gone mad! Either way, listen first thing in the morning and last thing at night, perhaps using an automatic stop so that you can fall asleep with the affirmations still going. This is a powerful way to tune positive messages into your mind that in time will begin to cancel out the old stuff and replace it with newer, more dynamic thinking. A difference should be noticed at the end of a month. It should be noted that if you've been a life-long worrier or negative thinker it **will not** take a similar lifetime to change it. The more that you believe in it, the faster it will work for you!

Whenever we try something, it doesn't matter what it is we do; it only matters that it works.

Mission statement auto-suggestion

A good technique for programming your mind for success is to read your mission statement every morning and last thing at night. An audio tape auto-suggestion can be used for this, so that your mission statement is narrated instead of read. A good reason for doing this is that your mind is being programmed with your goals first thing in the morning and last thing at night. This gives a clear instruction to the subconscious to let it know what exactly you need to do in your life and what its job is to help you achieve it. There are no "ifs" or "buts" about it; your mind knows exactly what to do and it will help you to achieve it with this technique. I know of no more powerful way to program the mind for achieving goals.

All these techniques work; it's just a case of finding which ways work best for you. The technique of auto-suggestion has been ridiculed in various T.V. sketches over the years and I still have friends who make jokes about it now! But make no mistake; this was and still is a powerful way to begin to recondition your negative thought patterns.

Well, what are you waiting for? Put this book down and do it!

Learn to visualise

Actually, there isn't really anything to learn here at all; in fact there is nothing more to do with this than what you're already doing. You see, we all think in pictures anyway, even when we don't think that we are. We go in and out of daydreams all day long without really consciously paying much attention to them. It is at those times that we begin to program our minds with our thoughts. Sometimes our thinking can be negative and our thoughts angry, so that when we eventually snap out of the daydream state the negative program has been set up. If this is repeated every day then it starts to be conditioned and therefore becomes automatic, which can lead to anxiety and stress. A little daydream here and there seems harmless and is in most cases but quite often we begin to analyse our lives negatively when we do this. This is why we must learn to use this ability differently if want to keep ourselves in the best mental health.

You **must** begin to visualise positive outcomes on a daily basis so that he mind can see what you **want** to happen, rather than dreaming up totally negative consequences that will never happen! Not a day goes by without my doing some form of positive visualisation. This can be at break time at work, perhaps while waiting for a client, or last thing at night — it doesn't seem to matter when I do this. What matters, though, is that I actually **do** it. It also matters that **you** do it also. I know of no great man or woman who didn't mentally rehearse the outcomes they wanted for themselves. The world's greatest leaders and inventers are called visionaries, which means that they see the future through their own thoughts. Their powerful thoughts actually help to create the world we live in. They are often powerful visualisers who rehearse the outcomes they want to occur by using their daydreaming time to its full potential. Great generals who are noted for their strategies in battle are always good visualisers. However, the waking state of thinking must not be confused with the conscious mind. There is a big difference between thinking with your conscious chatter and what I am talking about. What I am talking about is sitting or lying down with your eyes closed and mentally visualising an outcome that you want to occur. This is not worrying about it; this is mentally running through a situation and looking at the appropriate behaviour needed to get the job done.

By running through some different outcomes in your mind, you are then able to have a fairly good idea of what will happen if you do X or Y. Instead of doing something blindly you can now visualise the scenario and see how it ends. You will also be able to see what will happen if you use a certain type of behaviour. This easy technique can prevent major mishaps and personal disappointments from occurring where a lack of planning would have been the real cause. I use this technique quite extensively whenever I need to be on top form for something. Most people do the opposite, though. If they have a driving test coming up, for instance, they make themselves nervous by mentally running bad thoughts about themselves failing the test in some ridiculous manner. This is then repeated in their minds every day until the day of the test. This then often becomes a self-fulfilling prophecy, which actually occurs because they programmed it into their minds for it to happen in a similar way as they had imagined. Then they usually say something like "I knew I'd fail. I have no luck". Luck had nothing to do with it; what played a big part in the outcome was they way in which they used their powers of visualisation beforehand. People do this all the time whenever they start a new job or do something different. This is also a characteristic of the conscious mind thinker whose mind is always "helping" to show them the hidden dangers. The more a person replays the thoughts of a scenario going wrong in their mind, the more they begin to convince themselves that whatever they're thinking about is difficult or even impossible to do. Very soon a feeling of dread can be installed and then the situation can become like a phobia. It usually takes around a month to install it so that it becomes an automatic feeling, which is associated with the thought. When this happens the person only has to think fleetingly about whatever it was they were thinking about for the negative feelings to envelop them. At this point all wise thinking has gone out of the window because the feelings associated with it have taken over and any common sense has gone too. Every day in my office I see people who do this. Their lives are one big worry or drama brought about solely by their negative thinking.

Use your mind in the way it was designed to be used: powerfully, totally and wisely.

The fact that my clients do not want these bad outcomes to occur is irrelevant since, because they are focusing on these negative thoughts, their minds think that they are goal-setting. Their minds think that they **want** this to occur by virtue of the fact that they are focusing so much attention on it! If you feel over-anxious about any situation that really isn't dangerous then you are probably doing this too. This is such a common pattern that I think most people do it for at least one thing in their lives about which they have strong feelings. Think about it: do you have something coming up which you are dreading? If you have, what this means is that you have started the process of negatively programming your mind in this way; seeing an outcome you don't want to happen and using it as if it is a certainty about to happen. Let me tell you, if you do this in your head it **will** become a reality! You will **make** it so.

Even though you may have done this all through your life, it can be changed with a little effort. The only challenge that you might encounter is that the feelings you have now conditioned with this thought are pretty strong so that, even though you want to change, you may feel a little scared about doing so. This is only natural, because even though people can come to understand that it is their own thoughts about the situation that frighten them and not the actual situation itself, the fear seems real.

How many times have we imagined things to be frightening, only to find that they really weren't that big a deal after all? We blow things so out of proportion sometimes that when they don't happen in the way that we imagined them we sigh a huge relief. Once again, this form of negative thinking is another adrenalin-releasing thought pattern, which causes pH fluctuations and opens us up to the potential for disease. We must avoid using it.

Is there a better way?

Come on, you know me better than that. Of course there is! The idea that if you think and re-think the negative thoughts that you have about some impending situation you may actually prevent it from happening is both unrealistic and ludicrous. Some people think that by thinking about it in this way you may actually save yourself from the embarrassment, hence preventing the nightmare scenario from occurring in the first place. Believing that by doing this that this is actually helping you "see the reality" is simply not true as what you focus on **becomes** the reality. So we must change it around so that you are now focusing now on what you **do** want to happen. The way we do this is by using a simple but very effective mental rehearsal technique, as outlined next. The best time to practise this exercise is when you are quietly alone, without any disturbance. You can even do it in bed because then your subconscious mind is being reprogrammed while you sleep! Plus it will probably help you drop off to sleep. Also, remember to start the mental movie just **before** the behaviour you want to change. Do it twice a day for two weeks for maximum effect and then once a week from then on to keep it going. This begins to condition your mind for success rather than failure. The benefit of doing this exercise is that you will now have a reference in your memory bank of yourself doing it successfully, which can be used even though it hasn't occurred in reality. Remember that a thought is just a thought anyway. This simple mental rehearsal technique has been used by athletes the world over whenever they need to build self-confidence.

To mentally rehearse the outcomes that you want is to plan the events that will then occur because of that.

Future Behaviour Rehearsal Exercise

1. Identify the behaviour that you want to change or improve upon and remember a time or situation where you experienced it. Close your eyes, breathe easily and relax.

2. When you are relaxed you may begin to imagine yourself in the situation you want to better at in the future. You may want to imagine that you are a director of a movie and you are in control of it. The latter part is easier for the visual thinker but is not essential.

3. When you are ready, start the mental movie, watching yourself acting the way you want to act, in the situation you want to improve upon. Watch yourself in that movie walking, talking and acting in the way you would like to act in the situation instead.

4. See yourself as relaxed, assertive and confident or whatever you think is appropriate, as you would rather be, and run it through

until you're completely satisfied with the way you performed. When the movie is through, make the screen go blank.

5. Take a deep breath and relax. Now, start the movie again but, when you feel ready, float out of your director's chair and into that body in the screen. Stay in the body and run through the movie, see through the eyes of that person (the other you) in that movie with that new behaviour.

6. Notice how you sound and pay attention to any feelings you are experiencing at this time. If at any time during this you feel any tension or discomfort, just float back into the director's chair and change anything you have to, to make it more acceptable for you. If it's O.K., run it right through until you're satisfied. Do Steps 5 and 6 twice.

If an athlete were to start a race without any mental preparation, the outcome would be in the lap of the Gods. I can usually tell which athletes have best mentally prepared for a race when they say prior to a race "I hope I do well". If an athlete says this it tells me that they haven't mentally rehearsed the race through properly beforehand, seeing themselves winning the race. The word "hope" is used as a "get-out" clause because they aren't really sure of success, and that's because they haven't prepared themselves fully and don't want to embarrass themselves. People do this so that if they don't win, they have an excuse. They do not want to sound over-confident, as if they might put a curse on themselves if they do, by "tempting fate". They might have trained hard enough but if their mind is not right this will be the deciding factor in whether the race is won or not. The person who is the winner of the race does not put his faith in hope but rather puts their faith in him or herself. The winner does not believe in fate but rather that winning is their destiny. They also understand that destiny can only be achieved by training not only the body but also the mind. Prior to the race the winner says "I am going to win, put your house on me!". This is the attitude of the person who has properly mentally prepared for the race. This person night after night mentally rehearses winning the race many times in their head — so many times that they can actually feel what it feels like to win.

I was watching the World Games from Edmonton in Canada on T.V. the other night and I heard an interview with British decathlon athlete Dean Macey. Dean had just jumped a new personal best in the High Jump of over seven feet. The amazing thing wasn't the fact that he had jumped so high but it that he said that he hadn't physically practised it for over three hundred days. All he had done was mentally rehearse it! If this is not testimony to the power of our minds, I don't know what is.

Many other people in different jobs use this simple mental rehearsal technique when preparing to do something important. These include comedians, singers, surgeons, athletes, politicians, guest speakers, army generals and even everyday people who want to better themselves. It's no surprise, then, to see that the best performers in the world use this powerful technique.

Don't plan your own downfall!

Your mind is a goal-oriented machine, which tries to achieve what you focus on. The reason why it does this is because your mind doesn't know the difference between what you do want and what you don't want. If you focus on a negative consequence, your mind will think that you want to achieve this and will help you to achieve just that. Your mind thinks that you're goal-setting! Reminding yourself of a possible negative consequence may seem a sensible thing to do but rarely do these things actually come true. If they do it is probably down to our own doing. If it **is** a genuine thing to watch out for, you will know the difference, because your subconscious wisdom will let you know. As you begin the shift from using the conscious mind to using the subconscious wisdom as your guide you will find that the dramas that used to plague you will no longer exist. You will also find that any challenges that do come up you will be able to deal with in a relaxed, capable manner.

So, you must not plan to fail. Whenever a situation comes up, whether it is a new experience or an old one, in which you need to perform well, the mental rehearsal technique that was outlined earlier is the key to making it a better outcome. All that you are doing is using the same mental rehearsal technique that all successful men and women have used both past and present. You don't have to reinvent the wheel; just reinvent your thinking!

Don't just sit and think

This is a common problem that I see nearly every day in my office. People sit at home and think about themselves. When we sit and just think about our lives and ourselves we begin the process of self-analysis. For some reason, whenever we do this we only come up with negative stuff. I don't know why this is but it is true nevertheless. When people think too much, their mind starts to look for what's wrong in their lives and will **always** find something. When you look for what's wrong in your life you will always find something: I guarantee it. Whether that be your looks, your body, your partner or whatever else, you will always find something negative when you look. This needs to be avoided at all costs as it is an unhealthy way of using your mind, which can only bring about one result: misery! If the only thing that happens when we do this is that we make ourselves miserable then it doesn't take a genius to know that we have to stop doing it.

A client said to me the other day "But how do I stop doing it?", to which I answered "It's easy — you just stop doing it". He was surprised by my answer, as he thought that it would take some sort of big effort or crazy technique to shift it. You see, when we start to make decisions in our life often we are then able to make decisions about which behaviours we don't want any more. We just **decide** to stop doing them any more. It's as simple as that: once that you make a decision to change something that you are consciously doing then it is easy. If it's the right thing to do, then decide to change it. There are no "ifs" or "but what ifs"; if it is the right thing to do for yourself and for all concerned, then just do it. When I make a decision and I believe in that decision then I instantly change whatever it is that needs to be changed, whether that be myself or a circumstance in which I am involved. So if you have a habit of sitting and thinking a lot, know this: no good can come from it, and in time it will manifest itself in some negative manner, such as finding fault with yourself or your life or some other worthless mental exercise. This must be stopped at all costs; it is not only a waste of your time but it will **never** yield anything of positive value for your life.

Your mind will create havoc if you just sit there and think; you must exercise it every day and rest it through relaxation.

Take the example of Helen. Helen was a self-confessed depressive who, when she came to see me, said that she had no self-confidence. During the course of the first session it came to light that she spent many hours just thinking about herself and life in general. In this time of "self-awareness" she had come to find out what all her faults were. These faults were nothing more than negative thinking brought about by her "self-awareness" time. While analysing her life in these periods she began to literally pick her life apart, starting with her looks, then going on to her body, her intelligence, her family, her husband and lastly her friends. In time she was able to find faults in all of these areas and had turned thoroughly miserable in the process. Nothing that was said to her or done for her had any effect, as day after day she would start the analysis again. By the time she came to see me, Helen was a very unhappy and confused person indeed. She had begun to question the "meaning of life", and that is the question to end all questions! I am asked that question quite often when I am working. I wish I knew the answer, because if I did I would tell you. I have only my own theories which, I am sorry to say, are private! The first step to recovery for Helen was to stop sitting and thinking and begin to find something else to do in her life. Her life had begun to become very boring and a real drag for any person who knew her. She was hardly the life and soul of the party. In time, though, she began to change her thinking patterns into those of self-appreciation and adopted a new, more dynamic lifestyle. She took the time that was wasted before over analysing and started to build herself a life containing more activities and fun. She stopped sitting down and thinking about life and started actually to live her life. She set out her goals to give her life direction and began to live her life purposefully. She began to use the philosophies of this book and became a happy person for the first time in years. Not only did she feel good, but her family life improved dramatically also once she got out of the habit of sitting down and thinking about herself all the time. This story is testimony to how with the right effort we **can** change our lives around dramatically. So can you!

It must be said that if you need time to reflect and spend some time on your own, there are plenty of ways to achieve this without using the conscious mind. The ways I recommend are:

1. **Yoga**: This not only relaxes the mind but also helps to improve flexibility and muscle tone. This great "two in one" formula is ideal for the time-restricted individual who needs the "quick fix". Good results can be achieved in three half-hour sessions a week. Yoga classes and videos are available everywhere. What are you waiting for?

2. **Meditation**: A great mind-relaxer which usually lasts for an hour or so and can bring about a more peaceful personality for the person who learns it. As above, there are many classes, tapes and videos available to help you. Just look and you will find them.

3. **Self-hypnosis**: A wonderfully quick method for opening the doorway to the alpha state. In this state positive affirmations are more powerful and, with practice, trance can be induced in less than ten seconds. Check out my self-hypnosis induction in Chapter 8. Self-hypnosis videos and tapes are readily available everywhere to help you get started; just look and you will find them too.

Don't let miserable people influence you

Beware of negative people; they come in many guises. I was walking along the sea front the other day and I began to notice the different T-shirt logos people were wearing. You can learn a lot about a person's mindset by what is written on their T-shirt. Here are a few genuine examples I came across that day, giving away the personality type of the wearer:

- SAME SHIT, DIFFERENT DAY
- PSYCHO BITCH
- SMOKE DOPE
- I DON'T GIVE A F**K.COM

If you know a person who wears such clothing or similar stuff, beware as they are not the type of person who will help you to achieve your goals.

It's a sad fact that there are people out there who will always try to influence you negatively. People will always tell you that you shouldn't do certain things and try to keep you at their low level of achievement. These narrow-minded conscious mind thinkers use the same inept conscious mind that they use for their own life to try to influence yours. The same "scared to do anything different" mindset of that individual is then pushed on to you, in a vain attempt to keep you like them. People will always try to push on to you their negative opinions about everything, including what you should or shouldn't do. This "reality check" from them is nothing more than an attempt to control you in some way. Do not allow people tell you what you can or can't do, as just because **they** cannot do something doesn't mean that **you** can't. Just because they failed, they want to believe that nobody can do it either and that is why they try to talk you out of doing certain things; if you succeed then they will look ridiculous. This is predictable, though, as most conscious mind thinkers think that they are helping you to "see it as it is" but in reality it is actually **them** seeing it as it would be for **themselves** if **they** did it.

Quite often people mean well when they say "Don't have your hopes too high". What they fail to understand is that with their mindset it would be true but with the new mindset that you are putting into place you are far more likely to succeed than them. The conscious mind thinker lives in a world of self-doubt; this is the nature of the beast. It is predictable, then, that they doubt us as well as themselves, so don't be surprised or offended when they do so. Expect it but don't accept it. Throughout history, whenever great inventors embark on new ideas there have always been doubters who tell them that their ideas won't work. There has been a common theme historically that when a person does something out of the ordinary, people laugh at them. It is only when whatever it was is achieved by them and finally actualised that people will give them credit. Expect them to do the same with yourself. They act as if they are actually trying to save you the embarrassment of failure but in reality you only fail if you don't try. Take their doubt and make them eat their words; do whatever it takes for **you** to succeed.

So don't let these miserable people influence you, as what they say is their **opinion**, not fact. Whenever somebody tries to force an opinion on me that is negative I reply with either "In your opinion" or "That must be awful for you, thinking that". Usually people look bemused whenever I say this as it quickly points out that I have very different opinions to whatever they said. You see, people say things to us all the time as if what they say is an incontrovertible fact. Most of what they say are actually only their opinions. If somebody says to me that somebody is a horrible person I never believe that opinion as, without knowing that other person, how could I accept that? People say things like that a lot and some even get pleasure from doing so. This negativity is not only unpleasant for the person receiving it but also it robs the person giving it of their true spirit. I find that people get into the habit of slagging people off when they are in company, quite often when the other person has left the room. Usually the people who do this are insecure and need to do it to bolster themselves up by making somebody appear to be less than themselves. Whenever I go into companies to do workshops I usually find that there is always one person there who is the butt of the jokes; there's always one who gets picked on. This "harmless fun" can be psychologically damaging to the person on the receiving end, as they will begin to lose their self-confidence. The bully who tries to make him- or herself bigger by putting somebody down is the one with the **least** self-confidence.

If you do this, you must stop it **now**; you don't need to do it. And if you have had a habit of moaning or slagging people off, you must stop this too. It is shallow and negative and you don't need to do it. Try this instead; **go for a week without saying anything negative about somebody**. That's right, a whole week. I promise you that by the end of the week you will feel marvellous! You will feel a lot more peaceful, energetic and you will want to keep doing it. You will also become a nicer person and in time you will gain more friends. People will warm to you and trust you. Also, don't be part of negative gossip-spreading which may damage a person's character. Except in cases of real danger, keep your thoughts to yourself.

Every negative thought robs your body of energy so choose your thoughts carefully or they will tire you out!

Become less judgmental

For years I have had the natural ability to see through the eyes of another person, figuratively to step into the body of the person concerned. Being able to do this has given me a compassionate tolerance for the people I meet where others seek to judge them negatively. I hear people slag off others they don't **really** know. They **think** they know them, based upon what they **believe**. Whenever I meet somebody who, in other people's opinions, is not good enough I immediately mentally jump into their minds and bodies. This may seem a little strange but when you don't do this whatever you think after that is just a conscious mind evaluation and opinion. That is why, if ten people speak to just one person, every person would have their own unique opinion of that person. It is only when those ten people get together and discuss that one person that the dominant one of the group will try to manipulate the mindset of the group. All of them cannot be right, can they? They are only right in themselves, in their own minds. This technique of joining somebody else's viewpoint is a powerful way to help us understand people who are not the same as us and it can give you a whole new viewpoint and compassion for that person. I have had this ability for as long as I have known, but it wasn't until some time ago that I came to read that some people were touting it as a learnable skill. It wasn't until then that I realised I was already doing it. You can learn this too and it can help to improve our understanding of others to the point of enlightenment. There are always two sides of the coin and once we allow ourselves the possibility that our negative opinions are nothing more than judgements then we begin to grow both spiritually and as a whole person. The other day I heard a guy who was slagging off a homeless man who was begging in the street. This guy didn't know anything about the homeless man yet still he began to rant outrageous self-righteous opinions about him and he only had his preconceived judgements to back them up. Don't fall into the trap of bitching about other people just because other people are doing it. Have compassion for your fellow man, no matter who they are, as you could be in their position some day.

I use a simple exercise every day automatically to be less judgmental and more understanding of others. Even when somebody has done something bad to me and I'm annoyed, it still works. It doesn't mean that I am a doormat and every time somebody does something bad, such as steal my car or my stereo, I am happy about it. Not at all; but what it does do is allow me to be less self-concentrated and feeling like I'm a victim. Even if that person stole my stereo for money to buy drugs I can still feel for that person, as I do not see it as a personal attack; rather I see it as part of the negative cycle that the person has made for themselves. Having the ability to use this different perceptional viewpoint has allowed me to make friends with all types of people of all races and cultures. I remember reading once that Ghandi used this very same technique for successfully negotiating differences that needed his wisdom. Use it yourself too and join the ranks of the wise.

The following exercise is for understanding the people we meet. Using this technique we can start to bring about a new understanding of why people behave as they do, which will help ourselves mature and grow with that wisdom.

To understand the fact that we are all unique is not enough. We must live by that fact. In the same way as we are entitled to our opinions, others are entitled to theirs. Be at peace with that fact and you will find that you will take another step towards greater wisdom.

"If you judge people, you have no time to love them."
Mother Teresa

Understanding People Exercise

1. **You are now in first position, which means that you are being yourself in your own body and mind. This is your normal everyday viewpoint in life. It might help to close your eyes to do this exercise.**

2. **Now think of a person with whom you may not get along with or are angry with and run a movie of a past experience where you didn't get along. Run that movie from first position.**

3. **After you have run the movie, think about the other person, their past and the type of life that they have had. After that, imagine floating up and into the body and mind of that other person, which is second position. See through their eyes and think through their mind and run that same movie through again.**

4. **What did you learn? What do you now understand? Now float out of the other person's body and take a neutral viewpoint (third position). Run the same movie through again, watching both yourself and the other person, totally detached.**

5. **After watching the whole situation several times through these different viewpoints, ask yourself this question: "What have I learned from this?". Review what you have learned.**

After you have done this exercise a few times you will start to do it automatically in your life and then it will just become a natural part of you.

There may be times where you don't want to forgive somebody or you don't want to see things through their perspective, and that's up to you; it's your choice. Maybe you don't want to think that there could be a valid reason why somebody did what they did and you choose to dismiss any other data that isn't what you believe. That's your choice. Remember this, though you can only find true inner peace when you forgive those who do us wrong and you stop seeking validation for your thoughts.

Don't resent the wealthy

Do not seek the downfall of wealthy people and do not laugh when they hit hard times. Many people are jealous of others who are wealthy and wish that they were as rich. If you want to be rich you must seek out the world's wisest financial minds and study the tactics that they use so that you can become wealthy too. Every day I hear people complaining that the sports stars of today earn too much money, as if, if they were earning the same salary, they would give it all away to charity. Whenever I hear a story of a sports star earning a great wage, I am pleased for them. If a person can be well paid for doing something that they enjoy, then good for them. Why should it bother us what they get paid? It doesn't come out of my pocket and if I do pay to see them I have chosen to do so; nobody forced me to pay! The biggest difference between people who are wealthy and those who are not is that the wealthy take risks and the poor do not. Unless you're prepared to take some risks, you will always be at your current earnings level or thereabouts. Take the principles and philosophies in this book and you will be well on your way to becoming more wealthy, in both the financial and personal senses. Learn to enjoy somebody else's good fortune and not to resent it.

Chapter Eight

Principle 8: Enjoy Yourself!

That's right! I said "Enjoy yourself!". You **can** do it and you need to start doing it more. Lighten up, loosen up and cut yourself some slack. Stop being so bloody serious and enjoy yourself. It is my guess that if, prior to reading this book, you have spent long periods being depressed or unhappy, the chances are that you've been taking life too seriously. You've been too serious about your problems, too serious about yourself and too serious about most things. It's time to have some fun and actually use the information that is contained in this book and start to enjoy your life. It's time to use the exercises and philosophies described here to mould yourself into the fun, happy individual that you deserve to be.

If you don't enjoy your life, what it is point of it?

This is something that you should want to do anyway, regardless of whether you have read this book! Quite often, though, when clients come to see me complaining that their lives are no good, I ask them "When was the last time that you really enjoyed yourself?" and their mouths turn downwards. They normally say "I don't have time to enjoy myself. I have to do blah, blah, blah" and they wonder why they are not happy. You see, to be happy you have to do certain things in your mind and your body to produce that result. If you don't do anything to actually make yourself happy, I doubt you ever will be. You have to take time out from your routine for fun. Happiness needs to be worked at you can't just do one thing and hope that it's going to bring you happiness forever; you must cultivate it and build on it. You must take the specific steps to do whatever it takes to make sure that you stay happy. Some people's lives are totally taken over by doing things for everybody else and nothing for themselves. They put their lives on hold to sort out other people's problems. There is something wrong with the equation here. Does this sound like you? Do you think that the world will crumble if you are not there to prop it up? If you think it will, then you need to make some changes in your perceptions and in your lifestyle. You see, the world turned before you were born and it will continue to turn long after you are gone. I often see people who have become the victim of their own good nature. These people made the mistake early on of being a maid or butler to every whim of the people with whom they live or work. This good nature is always exploited, as the person on the receiving end starts to take on more and more responsibility for other people's problems. These good-natured types are usually easily to manipulate with guilt and pressure. The person who suffers from this guilty mind-set often retires to bed completely exhausted from the daily workload, without having time for his or her own pleasure. These manipulators, whether it be friends, family or work colleagues, love such good-natured people and thrive on passing over their responsibilities to their long-suffering "friends". Sometimes, when the good-natured person complains that nobody is giving them any help, the manipulator fiercely argues their point with a pre-rehearsed answer to embarrass or make the other person feel more guilt-ridden for bringing the subject up.

Do not allow yourself to be a doormat; your life is as important as anybody's.

Does this sound like you? If it does, read on or, if you are a manipulator, take heed. There is a very strong possibility that a person on the receiving end of such shabby treatment is ready to explode! Everybody has a limit or tolerance point. If this point is broken or exceeded, the person is like a grenade ready to explode. This can happen at any moment and can result in the person leaving you, having a nervous breakdown or even becoming seriously ill. If you say that you love such a person, you must change your ways before these things happen. If you are always a burden to somebody then it's time to take responsibility for yourself and stop putting your things onto other people's plates. Grow up and be pro-active as this other person will not be around forever to look after you.

If you have been on the receiving end of such people, it's time to teach them a lesson! You must refuse to succumb to their tactics. In the past, whenever we refuse to do the things that we have been manipulated into that are other people's business or responsibilities, there is always a challenge. The other people will complain no end and try their best manipulation tactics on you in order to make you yield. At this point you have to be firm and strong. Enjoy your new-found confidence, which will explode when you start to take charge of your life. All the time I see people who for years have been like doormats and as a consequence have not been happy in their lives. You must stand up for yourself and challenge the patterns of your life that in the past were dictated by the lazy manipulators.

When you make the decision to take charge of your life and change from being the passenger on the bus with the manipulators deciding what direction your life takes, to becoming the driver of your own bus with the power to change to whatever course you wish, your life will become dramatically better.

Don't worry about rocking the boat, as this boat needed rocking years ago! The patterns that have been allowed to manifest in your life today should have been nipped in the bud at the start, but they weren't, and whenever you try to change somebody else's patterns of behaviour there will definitely be some conflict along the way. But it's worth it; it's time to put yourself first now and start to enjoy yourself and do the things that **you** really want to do! They'll just have to live with it. I have seen so many people who have been to see me with depression because other people have taken a liberty with them.

Take the example of Mary. Mary was married with three children aged 8, 13 and 20. She worked part-time in a local shop, as well as being the chief homemaker, maid and chef for the whole family. Mary's husband worked at the local steel works and liked to go to the pub with his mates most nights. Mary's children always seemed to have some kind of drama going on that she had to sort out and make all sides happy. These dramas occurred on a daily basis and were totally taking over any spare time Mary had. This impossible scenario was made even worse by her husband's apathy, as his answer to any request for help was always the same: "Well, I've been at work all day". Because Mary had never challenged her family, or if she did she did it with so little conviction, this sorry state of affairs was allowed to continue and become just the usual daily practice. Mary had no time for herself in this situation and after some wild outbursts, which were out of character for her, she came to me suffering from stress. These outbursts were pure frustration after many years imprisoned in a life of drudgery. Mary had two choices: either she could try to put up with what she was allowing to happen to her in her life and remain stressed and unhappy or she could make a big decision to change her life. If she were to continue what she was allowing to happen, she would never realise her true potential or live her dreams. Her fear of being different to her normal self and what other people's reactions were going to be were the biggest obstacles she had to conquer. I taught Mary that all fear is just thought and how by changing thoughts we can change from thinking like a victim and move in more self-confidence. I also taught Mary how to change her physiology to that of a confident woman rather than a doormat. That family were in for a shock as Mary began to integrate the principles you have also learned to bring about the necessary mental shift from weakness to power. A month later and Mary's family had begun to realise that things weren't going to get back to how they had been so they had to make the necessary changes in **themselves**.

Sometimes when we are pushed too far, we snap, like the metal bar that's been bent so many times back and forth that it won't go back into shape any more. If you've had this experience then you know what I'm talking about. The same thing happens when people are in abusive relationships; they hit a point and the metal bar snaps and it can't go back into place. The limit has been passed; how far that limit is, is entirely up to the individual. Some people will go on for years, suffering from mental and physical abuse, hoping that the abuser will change their ways, before they say "No more", while others will terminate a relationship after the first time. It really is down to the individual and the strength of personality that they have. Have the strength to say "no!" and keep saying it until it sinks in. If you are in a new relationship or have recently became a parent then the boundaries must be made at the beginning. It's much easier to maintain the trend if it is the same at the start rather than changing half way through.

When we do everything for everybody we are not helping them; we are in fact actually crippling them and taking away their self-confidence.

If, for instance, your child will only eat sweets and you give into that whim, you will have to prepare yourself for **big** problems in the future. When you give in, you teach your child that they have control over you. Kids quickly learn this, even before they can talk, so you had better set up some rules quickly. The same happens with relationships; if you allow your partner to cheat on you, they will do it time and time again because you have taught them that it is O.K. to do so. Have some rules and discuss them with your partner when it looks as if your relationship is going places. Do it at the start and be specific: "If you cheat on me, X is going to happen".

If you allow yourself to be walked on by friends and family or your partner they will continue to do it because you have taught them to do it. Every time they do something and you allow it, what you are unwittingly saying to them is that it is O.K. to do so. Ponder this:

What would happen if you died tomorrow; what would they do? They would have to cope and they would have to do everything for themselves. It's time to shock people and begin to show them a whole new you. You see, by doing everything for everybody else you are not actually helping them anyway. You are actually crippling them by not letting them learn and grow as a human being. It's time to do the right thing for all concerned and stand up for yourself. What's the alternative? What would you really like to be doing in your free time? What hobbies or interests would you love to be doing instead of cleaning up everybody else's mess?

Rarely when speaking to people do I hear that they are truly fulfilled in their lives. Most people spend so much time and energy planning for later life that they forget to enjoy the life they're living right now. People put their lives on hold, thinking that when they retire they will then have plenty to enjoy, but I say: "Why wait?". Make the effort to enjoy yourself **now**. Enjoyment shouldn't be something that stops when you're 21 or when you get married and start again when you retire. There's a whole big chunk missing in the middle of this equation. It starts by learning to enjoy your life again. Take a holiday to Disney World and be a big kid again. Don't limit yourself with pre-conceived notions of time scales with regard to your age. You can be old at 30 or young at 80. It's up to you; it's your choice.

You must relax!

This important rule of life is often missed out because of excuses such as lack of time and the like. You will never find time to relax; you must **make** time. You must set aside a little bit of time every single day to do this for yourself. Relaxation is such a big part of physical and mental wellbeing that to miss it out is actually dangerous to your health. When we relax this is the time that our bodies repair the tissues that are affected by everyday living. We need to relax in order to recharge our batteries as when we don't do that it's like driving a car constantly at one hundred miles per hour. At some point that car is going to overheat and when it does, you know you're in trouble. A lot of people think that they relax every night in front of the T.V. but this is not the case. Television is entertainment and not relaxation; if you were able to see your facial expressions as you were watching, you would see yourself going through lots of different emotions. We must create a habit of daily relaxation even if it is for only 15 minutes a day. You will find that you will feel mentally sharper and have more energy to do the things that you need to be doing when you use a relax time. A great way to achieve a good, deep state of relaxation is by using self-hypnosis.

Next is my easy self-hypnosis routine that I use every week for myself and that I also teach to my clients. I do it about twice a week in order to clean my mind and reduce any stress build-up. It's a fast way to bring about immediate relaxation. Do not worry about entering hypnosis, as **you** control how deep you go and for how long; no, you **cannot** get stuck in hypnosis!

Without proper relaxation, we begin to grind to a halt. We cannot function as well as we would like and we spend more time achieving less. When we use relaxation as an unforgettable part of our lives, we can reverse this trend.

Steve's Self-Hypnosis Routine

Prior to trance, decide for how long and how deeply you want to relax. Say it out loud or in your head — it doesn't matter which — but do this so that you can program a wake-up time. If you do this you should awaken around the exact time that you chose. Any suggestions you want to be absorbed by your subconscious mind can be read or spoken out loud at this point. Decide what you want to gain from this self-hypnosis session and then:

1. **Take a deep breath, hold it and count to three, then slowly release your breath. At the same time as you breathe out, close your eyes and relax.**
2. **Allow the whole of your body to sink down and become heavy. Imagine that you are going into deep hypnosis and that you are becoming more deeply relaxed. Tell yourself that you are becoming more and more relaxed.**
3. **Let your breathing become slower and deeper and imagine that you are going deeper into hypnosis with every outward breath. Tell yourself that you are sinking deeper and deeper, until you reach a level at which you feel comfortable.**
4. **Use some form of visualisation — perhaps a holiday or fantasy place — and just relax; or if you want to improve some behaviour, you can use the Future Behaviour Rehearsal exercise in Chapter 7. Auto-suggestion can also be used at this point.**
5. **When you are satisfied that you have benefited from the relaxation or have programmed your mind with the new information, you can count back from five to one and return to your normal waking state, having benefited from the trance.**

Never hope to make everybody like you; it's impossible

A common mistake that lots of people make is to try to make everybody **like** them. This impossible need is a sure bet for disappointment and self-misery. Instead of asking yourself the question "Why?" whenever people don't seem to like us, understand instead that it is a fact that we cannot make everybody like us. Whenever I meet somebody I don't know, I never try to change myself in order to please that person. What that means is that I don't change who I am. That doesn't mean that I don't use my rapport skills; my rapport skills are now a part of me! If people don't like me for whatever reason, I'm O.K. with it. I no longer try to analyse whether I did or said something wrong. I just accept the fact that not every body in the world will like me. In fact, the more that you try to force somebody into liking you, the more you lose your own self-identity and you will appear false, which is worse. People would dislike you less for being yourself rather than pretend that you're somebody you're not. The great motivational speaker Ed Foreman says that if you get over 50 per cent of the people that you meet to like you, then you have won a landslide! This is very true in life; as long as you are true to yourself and you are happy in your heart with the person that you are, then you are on the path to richness and it doesn't matter what other people think. Do not try to please everybody as it is not only impossible but exhausting to try to do. Do things to please yourself. This is not a prescription for selfishness at all but what it is is a new mindset that frees you from the mindset that **needs** approval.

Live your life to the full; you won't regret it when you depart this Earth

All the time, people hold themselves back from enjoying themselves by thinking that it will embarrass some other person. If you embarrass them, then they need to lighten up too! Do not worry that your voice may not be too great for Karaoke or that you can't dance like John Travolta. In any case, when you stop worrying about those things they will probably improve by themselves. The "What will people say?" attitude needs to be replaced by "So what?", and remember that what they think is their **opinion** and not a fact. Don't take yourself too seriously, and take some chances. Start to enjoy yourself.

The world's most successful men and women, who would rather try and fail rather than never try at all, you should also employ this mindset. It all boils down to thoughts again; the only thing that could stop you is your thinking and we have already covered that topic in Chapter 2.

Remember that your thoughts control the way you feel, so don't let your mind poison you.

Reframe your experiences

One way in which you can change your perception of yourself and the events in your life is to **reframe** them. What this basically means is that you change the meaning of a thought to see it in a more positive light. A simple everyday reframe could be when people say "Darn, the interest rates have gone up!". You could reframe that by saying "That's great news for savers!". It's about seeing a positive from the negative and changing it around to your favour. I do this all the time. For instance, if a client rings and cancels half an hour before an appointment I could get angry or I could use the time to my advantage and relax or do something else of positive purpose that I couldn't do before because I didn't have the time. It's taking a potentially bad situation and turning it into a good one for yourself by changing the meaning.

A simple reframe is one that I used in Chapter 1: changing mistakes into learning experiences. This simple but powerful reframe has given me the confidence to take risks and try out new ideas that in the past I would have avoided due to the fear of failure. The idea that making mistakes is a bad thing to do is a very limiting one, which can prevent us from ever taking chances in life for fear of ridicule. If nobody buys this book or it gets bad reviews, then is this book a failure? No it isn't; it's only a failure if I let the **thought** of that prevent me from actually doing the things that will actually help to sell it. Even if nobody buys it, it will still have been an incredible learning experience for me, from which I can only grow. You see, there can be no negatives from this. If, at the very least, I have the satisfaction of writing and publishing my first book, then that's still a positive start, upon which I can build. Even if the experts say that this book is the worst on the market, I can learn from their criticisms. At least I had the guts to do it! You must adopt the same mindset in your life if you want to be successful and live the best life ever!

Start to think about yourself in the same way. Think that nothing that you want to do could ever yield anything but a positive outcome; if you look for the positive in everything that you do, you will find something.

I remember that a few years ago my dream house came on the market. I had wanted this house for as long as I could remember but when it came up I was devastated to find that the price was too high. I was gutted when somebody else bought it but I vowed to work smarter and improve my business so that I earned more. I took a gloomy situation such as losing my dream home and turned it into a positive experience by using it to motivate me to make more money. How many times do things happen in our lives which at the time seem like a nightmare, only for some time later to become a godsend?

When I was 19, my father was killed in a tragic works accident. At the time we were all devastated and it took all of our small family pulling together to keep us sane. As bad as it was through that difficult time, our family grew stronger and became even more solid as a unit. I come from a small family where to lose one of us was a big chunk to lose but our family bond grew so strong after that tragedy that we now don't take each other for granted any more. We all now have a stronger loving bond and appreciation for each other that we didn't have before and we always look out for each other. You see, as bad as this tragedy was, we still managed to salvage some positives from it.

If you have ever lost a loved one, chances are that your life changed in some way after that. If the only thing that we learn from somebody's passing is to appreciate the gift of our life and that we need to live for today, then there is a positive to take from it. We should not be living in the past or living in the future either but we should be living in the present — the here and now. The past is gone and the future doesn't exist. Nobody can live in the future because it is always ahead in time; it is unobtainable. We must appreciate and enjoy our lives now, today! Even in the most extreme cases we find examples of people who are still enjoying and appreciating life even though they are having a more difficult time than most of us. Next is a letter I received by e-mail from an acquaintance who has now become a friend.

Hi Steve,
Thanks for your e-mail. I visited the site this morning and it is truly impressive. Thanks too for your good wishes. Whilst I cannot deny that this is a difficult time, I know that there are so many people worse off than myself in so many ways. Life is about enjoying what we have and living for the moment. I have two more holidays planned … .one with the kids just after Xmas, and one with the whole family in April. My life is completely stress free and in a perverse sort of way, this illness has freed me up. Some may take the view that it is a blessing … I can relate to that … .it is a part of who I am, and it is up to me to take all the positives I can from it. Believe me, there are so many positives to be found. I know that I am fortunate to have a good income and good family support and I feel for others who face cancer without these things. Hey … I am a lucky man. Look after yourself and keep up the good work. See you soon,
Regards,
Mike.

This letter shows the positive attitude of my friend who, in the face of this illness, was able to find some good out of his situation. I am happy to report that Mike is doing well and is still as positive as ever!

Look for the good in life and you will find it; look for the bad and you will find it too. Begin to reframe every experience in your life so that you look for the good in whatever it brings you. Ask yourself “What good can I find in this?” when things don’t go your way.

I’m sure you’ve had times in the past where you thought that your life was falling apart or maybe you have been in a situation where you thought it was the end of your world. Now that those bad times are gone, what learning did you get out of it happening to you? How have you grown since because of that? As you ask yourself those questions, really begin to accept that there is always a lesson in all of life’s ups and downs.

Something unbelievably positive happened to you today: you opened your eyes. Millions of others didn’t! Appreciate that fact!

Hope

Hope is when you don't plan something. People use the word "hope" all the time when they haven't planned something well enough and they put it into the lap of the gods. It's the get-out plan people use to excuse themselves for not putting the right planning into whatever they are setting out to achieve. If a person says "I **hope** I pass the job interview" what this means is that they are not 100 per cent sure that they have put in the necessary groundwork needed to do a great interview. The well-prepared person says "I'm going to do a great interview". The person who speaks and thinks this way has prepared both physically and mentally, with the latter being the bigger factor.

When we hope for something to work out right for us we are almost resigned to its inevitable failure. We are clinging on to a vague possibility of success, so that the onus is then taken away from us. The responsibility is then put on the thing itself rather than ourselves. When asked about things that they want to achieve, most people use the word "hope" as if to not embarrass themselves if things don't work out. Do not be afraid to speak in the positive whenever you are about to do something challenging, because when you do this it sends a message to your brain that switches it into confident mode. If I say "I hope", this sends a message to my brain of self-doubt, which then circles back to me, and it will definitely affect the outcome that I want to achieve. Even if I think and speak in the positive about something that I am going to do and it doesn't come off the way I planned, it doesn't matter. For every one thing that doesn't come off I will average twenty that will. If I were to compare the two mindsets — one of "hope" and one of "knowing" — the one of knowing would yield the higher returns. Hope might yield a 50-50 chance and knowing one chance in twenty of not being successful. If you are a betting person, which would you choose?

Do not hope. Plan.

You might think that this is not really a big deal, but ponder this. The most successful men and women of the world all think in this positive manner. They never say "I hope my new business works" because if they do, they are doubtful and they need to get back to the drawing board. If they do say "hope" it is only done as to appear not so cocky to the person asking the question, but inside they are sure. Personally I think "hope" is a weak word, which I rarely use. If somebody asks me about a new business idea that I am working on and enquires if I think that it's going to work I will answer " I have put a lot of work into it and I am confident that I can make it work", rather than "I hope so". In fact, the only time I might say the word "hope" is if I am in a conversation about Bob Hope, the late American actor! When people say "I hope it works out for you" what they are really saying is that they don't have any real faith in your pulling it off. **Show them that you can!**

You're not perfect — nobody is!

One of the great things about being a human is our ability to laugh at ourselves. I never pretend that I live a perfect life and I never say that by following these principles you will be a perfect person living on a constant cloud nine. To be honest, I don't think that I would want a life in which everything was perfect all the time, as wouldn't that be predictable? I see "experts" on T.V. preaching to people about where they are going wrong with their lives and how they should follow their examples. This is all good and well but the theory of something is always different to doing it in reality. I have met quite a few personal development "gurus" over the years and I can truthfully say this. They are just like me and you; they have "off" days; they still make bad decisions; they still get stressed some of the time; and they do not leave the toilet smelling like roses either! Some of the more self-righteous of the "be like me" brigade are usually not living the perfect life that they preach about. At least **we** admit that we get things wrong sometimes. It is very easy to sit on a T.V. show, criticise the volunteers who come on to share their problems and tell them where they are going wrong. It's very easy to give advice but do these experts live the perfect life that they tout? Probably not, and neither do I.

What I am presenting to you with this book is not a guide on how to live the perfect life but merely a set of principles which, when followed, will in my experience give you a happier and more fulfilling life with the least amount of stress and anxiety. I am not presenting myself as some whiter than white "guru" who lives life without ever screwing things up. I am just a person like you, looking to get the best out of life. So it's O.K. not to be perfect. In fact, it is more than O.K.; it's actually better not to be perfect because the thought of having to be perfect is a constant source of misery for a lot of people. I still find people, though, who strive for it and even though I am all for improving yourself to be the very best that you can be, there is an unhealthy side of seeking perfection. The person who demands perfection from either themselves or the people around them is doomed to live a life of constant disappointment and anxiety.

People take this to the extreme with regard to their physical appearance, with the example of crazy plastic surgery procedures and the use of anabolic steroids. The person using these means to try to achieve perfection is never truly satisfied and is always seeking to "improve" with more drastic measures. We read stories all the time where attractive men and women spoil themselves by undertaking dangerous surgical or chemical procedures in a vain attempt to achieve perfection. If happiness is experienced by such people it is only short-lived until more "faults" can be found. We really want to get away from this kind of mindset and start to understand that to strive for perfection is a big disappointment waiting to happen. Exercise is a great way to shape our bodies and give us self-confidence, as long as we don't become obsessed about it. I hear people all the time moaning about their physical appearance and pulling themselves down. Usually women do this with their bodies and their weight, always finding fault somewhere. They look at themselves in the mirror, trying different angles to see how they look, and then start to criticise themselves mentally. With men the body comes second to their hair. Baldness or greying are the focal points that cause much worry and self-doubt.

This type of negative "pulling yourself down" mental exercise needs to be stopped if true inner peace is your goal. This is nothing more than a bad habit that the person doing has formed by the repetition of the negative thoughts about themselves. If you have a habit of doing just that, understand that when you do this completely pointless mental exercise the same dumb answers occur every time.

Allow yourself to have an "off" day. Everybody has them, so it's O.K. when you have one every now and then.

The reality of life

Nobody lives a life without ups and downs, not even me. The difference is though when you live by these principles you have a more even up and down trend so that the downs aren't way down and they don't stay there very long. The principles described in this book when absorbed and applied will make your downs far less and your ups more constant but in no way promise a life on a constant high. The difference is when you are faced with life's dramas you handle them differently because of this new wiser mindset. Check out the diagram below which shows the two different mindsets. The centre line represents normal life, anything above it is exceptional.

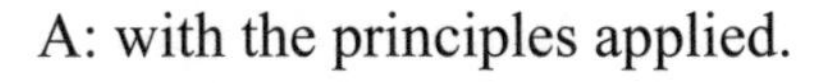

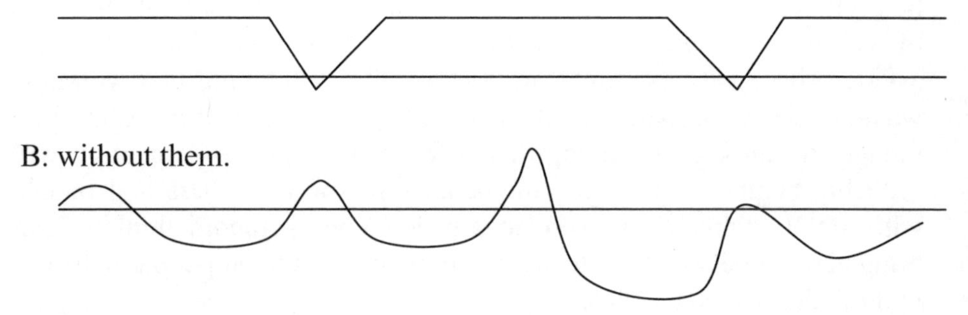

Stop mind reading

Stop mind reading; you don't know what they are thinking about you. You only **think** you know — there is a big difference. I have a lot of people who come to see me who suffer from mind reader's syndrome. Some people don't realise that they actually do it and realise only after I highlight it to them. This error in thinking is common in the conscious mind thinker and can cause much unhappiness. There is only **one** result that occurs for the person who habitually tries to mind read the people they know to gain insight on how **they** think about them. The result is that you will think something negative. In almost every case of working with clients who mind read, they come up with the same thing; they think that the other person is or other people are thinking something bad about them. Now, I don't know why this is but it is nevertheless true that when we try to think about how other people think about us in this way we always come up with something bad. This seems to make us search for evidence to back it up whenever we do this and we usually find it. So, whenever we do this, the only feedback that we will receive from our minds will be negative. With this knowledge in mind, then, it is not a good idea to use this form of mental thinking, to say the least.

If we will only receive one result (negative) then, unless we want to feel negative, we must stop this silliness now. Just because you may have been doing this for a long time does not give you the excuse to keep on doing it forever. The idea that we can step into another person's mind and find out exactly what they are thinking about us is not only ludicrous but also untrue. If it were true then it would make police investigations much easier, as all the detective would have to do is look into the eyes of the suspect and tap into their mind to find out the truth. If you were a contestant on the game show *Who Wants to be a Millionaire?* it would be even better still, as all that you would have to do is look into the eyes of the presenter and extract all the answers to the questions they were asking. These silly examples are just as silly as thinking that we know what people are thinking about us. The thing that you will probably find, though, if you keep on doing this is that your negative perception **will** probably begin to show in your behaviour towards others and people **will** start to think about you negatively. Your paranoid thinking can bring about a personality change in yourself whereupon people will start to think that you **are** weird.

The truth is that we don't know what people really think about us and when we **think** that we do, all we are doing is making a judgement based upon our intuitions and thoughts. We think we know what they are thinking, based upon how we would think if we were in their situation thinking about us. Crazy, isn't it? Using your mind in this way will never yield any positive results, only misery, so it must be stopped. It won't be hard to stop doing it, though; all you have to do is make a simple but big decision to stop doing it and if you ever find yourself doing it unconsciously, just remind yourself that you don't do this type of silliness any more. Every time you remind yourself in this way you are beginning to re-condition your mind so that in a short time you will find that you no longer do it or you may even forget that you ever did it. If mind reading yields only negative results then there is no point in doing it, is there?

Once I once had a young lady come to see me, suffering from low self-esteem. One of the things she believed that she could do was read the minds of the people she met. The problem was that whenever she "read" their minds she thought that everybody was thinking she was a horrible person. She was utterly convinced that she could do this but when I asked her to read my mind she confessed that she couldn't. The truth is that we cannot read anybody's mind; we can only speculate about what they are thinking. Sometimes the people we meet are having a bad day (they should have read *The Principles of Life*!) and they appear a little "off" with us. To the mind reader this is proof that the person doesn't like them and they store that information in their mental reference library for later evaluation. The person may have had a row with their spouse that morning but the mind reader thinks it is a personal attack on them and starts to mull it over. The key to surviving this silly circle is to not play the mind reader game at all and just let it go. Don't over-react and make it a big deal inside your head, imagining future problems with that person. Don't let your thoughts play tricks on you. If you over-react and start to act in a negative manner with that person you will start to get the results that you have **thought** about occurring between the two of you. Accept that the person may have their own problems and that the way they are acting is as a direct result of those factors. Always give others the benefit of the doubt. You are probably not the centre of their thoughts, even though you may think you are. They are probably having a bad day and are not attacking you personally.

Dull life?

If you are suffering from a dull life, you must take responsibility for that being the case. Life is as exciting or as dull as we make it. If you do nothing or wait for others to bring excitement into your life, you're going to be disappointed.

"We find that life is dull and boring primarily to dull boring people."
Ed Foreman

If your life has gone stale then it is up to you to do something about it. Whenever I say that to my clients, they usually say "But what can I do?", as if I am the oracle who knows exactly what they have to do in order to enjoy themselves! This is one answer you must figure out for yourself as I can't tell you what you would find interesting, can I? It's time to get the old grey matter working for you and start to think about what you can do to change your life from being dull. Do you bring your work home with you? Is work the main topic of your conversation when you're at home or when out socialising? If so, you are going to fall into the "dull life trap". I still have some friends who don't really know what I do. This is because I rarely talk about work. If your life is boring you cannot just wait there, hoping that something or someone will come along to change it. You must get off your butt and make it happen! There is so much to do these days that was simply not available years ago. There are opportunities to learn things now that was virtually restricted information years ago but now, with the availability of the Internet, we can access it in seconds.

Great lives aren't born — they are created.

What would you really like to do that you know would bring into your life real excitement? Even if you cannot afford to do the things that you would like to do, you could make it another challenge to raise the money to enable you to do so. You could make it all part of the excitement, as the build-up to doing something that you really want to can be exciting too. Whatever you do, don't leave it to the lap of the gods, because that won't work.

Don't let the weather dictate your happiness

Somebody once asked me how I knew that all this personal development stuff worked. I remember the day it truly dawned on me but it wasn't any spectacular event at all. In fact, it happened in my local supermarket! I was standing in line at the checkout, waiting to be served, when I overheard a conversation between two ladies in front of me. One was a shopper and the other worked there at the checkout. The two ladies were complaining about the awful weather and were quite annoyed by it. At this point I turned around and looked out of the window and I was surprised to see that it was pouring down with rain. I looked at myself and noticed that I had a coat on and that the coat was damp. I had put a coat on that day with out even noticing the weather. That was the point where it hit home. I realised my mind had become trained to be so positive that it had filtered out the fact that it was raining and just let me know that I needed to wear a coat. I didn't need to know that it was "awful weather"; only that I needed to put on a coat. And this still happens. I rarely notice bad weather. There are only some days when I put on a coat and there are some when I don't. I told you it wasn't dramatic but this story does show that when the mind is positive, you don't have to notice the negative. The positive mind can filter out the negatives so that we don't have to experience them as others do. Clever, isn't it?

It is unwise to have a condition set up in your mind so that, if the weather is not what you might have wanted it to be, you will be disappointed and upset. On a daily basis I hear people moan, using bad tonality, that the weather is lousy and that it is "depressing". How ludicrous is it to base our happiness on the weather? We have absolutely no control over the weather but we have total control over our happiness. People do this, though. They look out of the window and when they see rain they moan and write the day off as a waste and their whole physiology and tonality change to match their thoughts about the weather. They stomp around, moaning about the unfairness of it, as if it is some kind of personal vendetta. For me, I am always grateful when I wake up and see daylight, regardless of the weather conditions, as you can still find much beauty in all weathers, including rain.

Where I live in the North of England, we are blessed if we have a month of warm weather in the summer and the rest of the year it is usually cold or raining. The geographical location of where I live is not conducive to warm weather but there is still a large majority of people who get very disappointed when the weather is not what they want it to be. They live an unrealistic hope that one day the weather might change so that it will match their ideal, even though the location of the country in relation to the world makes it impossible. Do not pin your hopes or happiness on the weather. If you do, you will set yourself up for disappointment. Instead, start a new mindset that says the weather is not going to affect how you feel, and do not regard the weather as a factor in your happiness. It is an established tradition to talk about the weather when making small talk and to agree about the "terrible weather" but refrain from starting a conversation like that as it is pointless and a waste of your valuable brainpower. Install a new mindset that says that, regardless of the weather, you will be happy and will not wish for anything different. If it rains and you have planned a day out, do something different. Don't get angry and moan that the weather is out to get you. Instead, be proactive and devise a new plan of action to accomplish what you set out to do. To base your happiness on the weather is a ridiculous strategy, especially if you live in England. Make a decision that, whether it rains or not, it will not affect the way you feel or your happiness.

Value who you are!

What is your most valuable asset? Your car, your savings, your house or is it yourself? You are sitting on a multi-billion pound asset, which of course is yourself. This may seem a little unbelievable at first but, if one person can achieve it, it means that anyone can. We don't really know how much money we could potentially make but what I do know is that the belief system that we have will determine how far we go on that particular track. Valuing yourself means much more than financial power, though. What it also means is that your time is precious and what you spend your time on has got to be of value. So we cannot just let time slip through our hands as if we are immortal. We don't know when it's going to be: it could be tonight, tomorrow, next year or 80 years from now — we just don't know. But think about this: if you knew you were definitely going to die one year from now, how would you live the rest of your life? Would you stay at home and pick faults with your body? Would you get angry with bad drivers? Would you worry about travelling on a plane? Would you get all stressed about your job? Would you still hold a family grudge? Of course not. These things would not matter. What **would** matter, though, was living the remainder of your life being kind to yourself and appreciating your life to the full. There would seem to be little point in comparing yourself with some person from a magazine and making yourself depressed. It would seem so senseless as your time would be so valuable with every day becoming an opportunity to live fantastically. You wouldn't want to waste it by using silly, negative mental exercises that yielded no positive results. I'm sure you would want to leave a positive and lasting impression on the people you knew and those you met before you departed. So what I am saying is that you would truly value yourself and your time and understand that picking fault with your physical self is a pointless exercise. But rather than waiting for a scenario like this to happen why not live like this now?

You are your greatest asset. Value yourself and respect who you are. You are priceless as there is the only one of you in the world!

From now on I want you to begin to build yourself up rather than pulling yourself down. I want you to understand and know that there is no "magical" difference between you and the successful men and women on this planet. The only difference is that they have the guts to chase their dreams. They don't listen to the narrow-minded opinions of others. They do it regardless, and **that** is the difference. Now, I'm not suggesting that you should want to be a millionaire. All that I am saying is that if that is what you want to be, you can. I want you to begin valuing your health, your mind and your physical body, no matter what condition they are in. If you are in a position to improve your body physically, you should. If not, turn it into your advantage in some way. You are the only you that you have, so be kind to yourself. Be thankful for each and every moment you are alive, and appreciate the fact that you are. You might be sitting on a gold mine with an idea or business plan that if you took a little of your courage might come true. You are also valuable to the world, as when we absorb this knowledge and begin to use it as part of our wisdom we can help others who might need that wisdom. Begin to think about yourself in a whole new way. Start to understand that, as you feel better about yourself, then other people will feel better too. Know that, even by buying this book, you are helping my goal of tiger conservation, about which I am passionate. My long-term plan is to make enough money to buy or co-own a "big cat" breeding facility, which will help to keep tigers away from the threat of extinction. For that, I thank you for buying this book. So you are already doing some positive good in your life!

Be at peace with your little faults and don't try to change them all. The world would be a dull, boring place if everybody just acted in accordance with a given ideal. I like the fact that I have faults; they make me who I am. Whenever people meet me they will find that I am down to earth and human, just like them. Sometimes, when I get excited, I speak too fast and my words come out jumbled up. Rather than beat myself up about it, I like to think that people like that about me, and the fact that I do not try to portray myself as some sort of Superman who never makes any mistakes. I'm just like you: I still say the wrong things, I still lose my keys and I do have the occasional "Why me?" moment. We all have our little quirks and I like mine, as they amuse me. No doubt you have your own little quirks too and perhaps they annoy you or even others. So what? They have quirks too, don't they?

Choose happiness

Remember, it takes no more effort to be happy than to be sad, so you must choose happiness. Happiness is not out there waiting for you to collect. It is inside you now; it's a choice. It's a philosophy of living, thinking, behaving and breathing in a certain way and understanding that our behaviours and limitations are just thoughts and that a new life and new dreams are just a new thought away. Don't worry if it takes a little time to get there; you have the rest of your life to practise. Living the principles outlined in this book will take you there more easily and more quickly than waiting to win the Lottery which, by the way, I'm sorry to have to tell you, you're **not** going to win. Make yourself and your life the winning ticket and invest in yourself and begin to believe in yourself more now than you have ever done before.

Simplify your life

Begin to take all the clutter out of your life. If there are things still there from a negative past, decide to get rid of them. Change your house around, buy some new curtains and get rid of any old stuff that has memories attached to it. If something doesn't move you towards a more positive and fulfilling life, then why would you want to keep it anyway? You have learned from the past and it is time to move on. Focus on the things that mean the most to you and begin to make those things your priority. Move away from the influence of the conscious mind and go by your instinctual subconscious wisdom.

Life is nothing until we do something with it. Don't try to rush it and don't take on too much. Enjoy and appreciate what you have now, as it's the little things that make life so special.

Final word

The chances are that I don't know you and that we have probably never met. Even so, I still think what I am about to write is very relevant to you. All through our lives, things could have been better, things could have worked out better, people could have been better to us and some times we have felt as though we are failures compared to other people. I want you to know that even though you may have felt this way, **you are and always were good enough**. I want you to truly understand that we can only do what we can do but when we take a step out of our own perceptions and look for guidance from others, we are able to see a bigger picture. I thank you for taking the time to step out of your perception for a while and join me in mine. I want you to know that if nobody has ever believed in you throughout your life, you now have one person who does. **Me.**

I believe in you. I do not say this out of some kind of cliché. I say this truly from the heart.

I do hope that you have really taken the time to go through the information in this book and have tested out the various exercises. If you have not, you will not attain as good results as you could have achieved. These philosophies and techniques have been the cornerstone of the work that I have found to be most beneficial for myself and my clients with the aim of living a great life. Remember that, by itself, a book cannot change anyone but it can be the spark to get the fire started. Once the fire is up and running, you must maintain it, rather as you would maintain your car. You don't take it for one service and then say that it will work perfectly ever after that for life, do you? Of course not. You have to take it back for regular services — and the same applies to you. You must apply these principles and re-apply them over and over so that you never forget them. You must endeavour never to become complacent with yourself and to continue to strive for never-ending improvement for yourself with further personal development.

Live the best life ever!

Steve

NO DOUBT

Summary of Common Complaints and Treatment Strategies

Listed on the following pages are some of the most common complaints about which people come to see me. Although there are literally thousands of complaints that people have, it would take another full book to document them all. The treatment strategies outlined in the following pages can be adapted to your particular challenge because many of these challenges are caused by the same thing: thinking! So don't worry if your specific challenge is not listed. The treatment strategies shown below were chosen because they are far reaching so that you can relate to some part of them with your particular challenge. Whenever we have challenges in our lives we must treat the cause and not the symptom; if we treat only the symptom, a new one will be replace the old one. This is common in smokers where they stop smoking and start eating instead. One symptom is treated and a new one pops up in its place. The treatment strategies outlined next treat only the causes, which in most cases involve thinking. The symptoms in themselves are relatively unimportant as, once the <u>cause</u> is treated, the symptoms cannot exist and will then fade away.

The following treatment strategies are, in my opinion, the simplest and most powerful of all those I have used, and that is why I use them extensively for my clients. Of course, there is always more than one way to skin a cat, so if you find any better ways, please let me know!

Controlling your weight

This common complaint affects two main categories of personality. The first personality type is moderately overweight by perhaps only 12–24 lbs. This person is not obese but feels self-conscious about his or her body and perhaps feels a little embarrassed about letting people see the "real them" under their clothes. This person can usually hide their excess weight quite easily from other people as it is usually not so noticeable but they cannot hide it from themselves. This is more of an annoyance to the person rather than a health problem. More often than not I have found that it is a boredom problem rather than an emotional problem. As it says in Chapter 4, the mind needs to be stimulated or else it will look for something to give you a bit of "drama". The weight increase can often become your drama as your mind is screaming for something new to think about. The person who has this slight weight problem was probably once quite active and adventurous but now life has hit a rut. The same old things day in and day out provide no real stimulation so the mind creates a symptom to let them know it needs exercising. The past holds the clues for overcoming this problem; if you look at what you were doing back then and start to do those things again, you will reap the same rewards. If you look back into your past, to the days when you weren't over weight, you will find that you were doing things back then that were more stimulating and fulfilling. You didn't have time to get bored and rummage through the cupboards looking for unnecessary snacks to take your mind off your boredom. Back in your past, when you were thinner, did you even bother to focus on your weight or were you so absorbed with enjoying your life that you didn't have time to get bored? You need to go back into your past and see what you were doing back then and repeat that same strategy for your life now. The more time that you focus on your weight, the more it will be a problem. You need to focus on it **less**, not more. Do not worry that if you let go of your thoughts about your weight, it will sky rocket. In fact, it will reduce as long as you begin to put some other interesting activity in its place. Remember, in the past you didn't think about it and your weight didn't sky rocket back then, did it? The only time that you put on weight is when you begin to focus on it. Forget about your weight and focus on something better and your weight will fall off all by itself. Begin to take in some more exercise, not to lose weight, though, but because you need it and it's good for you. If you eat due to stress use the exercises and philosophies in this book to help you with that.

The next personality is the overweight person who is more than 24 lbs overweight and can weigh in excess of 300 lbs. More often than not, the person who suffers from this complaint is seeking something through eating that they cannot get through everyday means. With every behaviour that we have there is always a payoff for it somewhere down the line otherwise we would not do it. This could be an emotional need not being met, a lack of self-esteem, an overactive conscious mind, a defence mechanism, or even a lack of proper knowledge about good food versus bad. More often than not, though, the person who is overweight is actually quite knowledgeable where it comes to nutrition, even sometimes more so than myself. If a person is quite heavily overweight they usually have been on every diet and fad and have built up a sizeable knowledge base where food is concerned but cannot break free from the cycle into which they have conditioned themselves. A faulty belief system can also be in place whereby the person believes that they are "from a big person family" so that they are destined to be large. This negative belief is a powerful force that makes permanent change impossible until the negative belief is banished if this applies to you. Go back to Chapter 3 and read about beliefs and do the belief changing exercises too.

What is the payoff for this behaviour; what do you get out of it? Do not think quickly and say "Nothing!". The answer is not in the conscious mind or you would already know what the answer is. Relax, close your eyes and ask your inner mind "What is my payoff for overeating?". You may be surprised at the answer. Whatever the payoff is, ask this question, for example: "If my payoff is that it allows me to feel comfort and contentment, how can I have those things without having to over eat? What could I do instead to fulfil those needs that would be healthier for me both physically and emotionally?" Whatever the answer is, it will be coming from your wisdom, so it must be put into action right away with first a decision to do whatever it says and then a commitment to follow it through forever. Anything less than this will not work and you will be wasting your time.

If a lack of proper food knowledge is the case, I recommend the Atkins Diet as I use this with my clients and it does make weight come off quickly and people find it easy to keep to. The person who thinks that they can lose weight without engaging in some form of exercise is mistaken. Exercise is essential for the overweight person who really wants to lose weight. Without it, muscle will also be lost through the dieting process and the person will look ill. I have seen many people lose weight too quickly and without exercise and look terrible afterwards. I recommend exercising three times a week, gently at first and steadily increasing the intensity when you become fitter. Also, weight training must be undertaken to tighten up any sagging skin that may occur with dramatic weight loss. A loss of 2-3 lbs a week is easily achievable and sensible as a new lifestyle is now in place. A **permanent** exercise regime **must** be scheduled into the weekly routine and cannot be forgotten or put to one side. Not for a month or a year but for forever. You have to make the time in your schedule rather than seeing when you can fit it in. The person who thinks we can lose weight and maintain it forever without exercising is living on Mars. Come round my house later and I will sell you some fairy dust. As we all well know, there would be no free time for it if we didn't **make** time for it. As with the first personality type, you must begin to turn your focus away from your weight and concentrate on living your life the way it was meant to be. You must get into the habit of changing your eating patterns to eating three meals a day with a small meal at night, as we don't need a large meal after work when we are resting. The typical routine of the overweight person is to skip breakfast and have a large meal at the end of the day. We must reverse this habit and change it into having a good-sized breakfast and a small meal at night; do this and you will be well on the way to losing weight.

Make exercising second nature; like brushing your teeth, you never forget to do it. Install your new payoff behaviours into your psyche and repeat them until they are an unconscious habit. The same goes for the previous two elements: eating and exercising. The Changing Bad Habits Exercise outlined in Chapter 1 must be also used to associate pain with your unhealthy eating patterns.

Gambling

The compulsive gambler starts out looking for the short cut to wealth. There are two types of gambler. The first have an occasional bet where they bet what they can comfortably afford to lose and view those losses as worthwhile expenses for the entertainment they have received in return. The second type is the compulsive gambler who hates losing his or her money and seeks to recap their loses with further betting. These people are life-blood to the bookmakers who cherish these clients. Because the compulsive gambler hates losing money, they live in hope that one "big bet" will pull them out of the mess they are in and **then** they will stop. They constantly mull over the amount of money that they have lost and get stressed out about it. The thought of losing all that money annoys them so they try to win it back again via more betting. The challenge is, though, is that although they can logically see the nightmare they are in and the way it is wrecking their lives, they still enjoy the buzz of betting. The buzz overrides the negative side of gambling rather like the heroin addict wanting the fix. I've seen people lose their businesses, marriages and homes through excessive gambling and still gamble. The first step in solving this challenge is first to accept that all the money that you have lost is now **gone** and write it off as an expensive learning experience. You can never win it back but you can learn from your experience. The learning could be that all gambling is a mug's game and then make a decision never to gamble on **anything** again. When I say "anything", I mean it; not even the Lottery. You can't even chance one bet, just as an ex-smoker cannot chance having one cigarette. You must sit down and make the biggest decision of your life. You must decide never to gamble again in any form and make it a true **commitment** and not a wish. You also need to change the association of pleasure with gambling to that of pain; this can be achieved by doing the Changing Bad Habits Exercise highlighted in Chapter 1. The money is **lost** and you must accept that and there will be no big win to recap it all back. There is only more misery and more debt as a gambler. Ponder this: in a bookmaker's, how many windows are there to pay your money into? How many windows are there to pay out to? What? Are you still here? I thought you had a big decision to make!

Phobias

Many clients come to see me complaining that they have a phobia. In most cases, though, we find out that they do not but instead have developed a powerful fear of a situation or something. The word "phobia" is used loosely these days whenever people have strong negative feelings towards something. More often than not, in my experience, the fear is brought upon and increased with the repetition of negative thoughts which then turn into a phobia like reaction. The more the thought is thought in this negative manner, the more powerful the feelings associated with it become. When I was younger I had a very strong fear of closed-in spaces such as shopping malls and supermarkets. I would dread the thought of going to such places as I always thought I would have a panic attack while I was there. The more I **thought** about it, the worse and more afraid I would feel. I would sweat and my heart would race at the thought of going into such places, so I would avoid them. The way I cured this problem was that one day I made a decision; a decision to stop being afraid. I began to understand that it was not the shopping malls I feared at all but that it was my own thoughts. It was my **thoughts** about the situation and **not** the situation itself that was causing me to feel scared. I took my new decision and walked into as many crowded shops as I could and the funny thing I found was that without the negative thoughts the fear could not exist. That was the end of it. Mental rehearsal is the key for solving fear challenges as well as making big decisions.

True phobias, on the other hand, are an automatic response to a traumatic event occurring in our early childhood that is then coded into our nervous system and recurs whenever a similar situation arises. The key to changing phobias is to begin to change your perception with mental rehearsal and courage, as a phobia is not a logical challenge and no amount of self-talk will usually work. The phobia is locked in the subconscious mind so the feelings will occur automatically whenever an anxiety-provoking situation arises. The only way to change this in my experience is to get yourself relaxed and imagine yourself in the situation doing the thing that brings upon the anxiety state and instead imagine yourself doing whatever it is in a **relaxed** manner. Run the scenario through a few times a day, always seeing yourself acting in the way that you would **want** to act and behave in the given situation. You must begin to condition this new thought pattern into your mind with the repetition of this exercise, as an imagined scenario is just as powerful as an actual event. You must run this exercise through thoroughly three times a day for about thirty days to start to change your mind's perception of the challenge. For further information on changing phobias, check out the Future Behaviour Rehearsal exercise in Chapter 7. Also use the Changing Bad Habits Exercise for the thing that bothers you and use it to associate pain with **not** changing this behaviour. Finally, make a decision to face your fear; set a date and time in your mind and make a decision to do whatever it is regardless. The techniques above will give you the strength and confidence to make it easier; all you have to do then is show some courage! What's the alternative? Try T.F.T, Thought Field Therapy.

Stress

Stress is brought about by one thing and one thing only: **thinking**. You cannot feel stressed without thinking stress-producing thoughts — it's impossible. When we are suffering from stress it occurs when we take the whole of the events of our life and think about them at the same time. This causes a mental overload and adrenalin is then flushed into the body. The more a person thinks about their life in this way, the more stressed they become. Trying to solve one's problems by focusing on them all at the same time is the cause of this tension build-up. The individual who is going through this challenge feels like a coiled spring, ready to pop at any second. At this point all sense has gone out of the window and anything that is said or done is taken the wrong way. The person suffering from stress usually does not take advice too well and views it as criticism. Any little thing is analysed and blown out of proportion because there is too much information going into the mind at once. Paranoia can set in as the devious conscious mind is in full flow and firing on all cylinders.

However, there is a better way to deal with your thoughts which will help to put them into proper proportion. Whenever people are suffering stress they typically see and hear their thoughts in their minds as large, bright and loud. Whenever we do this it intensifies the feelings that we have, so that they become more powerful. What we need to do instead is to make them less intense by changing some of the properties of the thoughts. If we change the location, distance, colour and sound of the thoughts that are causing us to feel stressed, then we will change the feelings associated with them. When we do this we are then able to view the same events in our minds without the immobilising feelings of stress. This is a much better way to sort out the things that need your attention most and give you a valuable insight into the things that caused you to feel stressed. It lets you see them in their true proportions. You need to **relax** at this point with one of the relaxation techniques outlined earlier in the book. Invest in some relaxation music and play it as frequently as possible. Relaxation is the key to solving this problem and time must be set aside every day for it. It's not enough to say "But I can't relax"; you must learn to because if you don't, you will suffer the consequences. For a full explanation of how to change your perception of the stressful events of your life, check out the Stress Eliminator exercise in Chapter 2.

Panic attacks

Panic attacks usually occur after the symptoms of stress have been ignored. This seems to happen all by itself but it is actually built up by thoughts beforehand. After the first panic attack occurs, the worry begins where the person dreads it happening again. The thought of it happening again is replayed over and over until it becomes a conditioned feeling of dread whenever the thought is thought. The more that it's thought, the more conditioned it becomes, so that it is inevitable that the negative scenario will occur. When it obviously does occur, and it will occur because you have programmed it to do so in your mind, you then feel validated and say "I knew it would happen".

The fact that it happens again and again is due to the re-thinking of old memories of previous panic attacks and then imagining future scenarios of seeing yourself in some kind of negative imagined scenario. Imagining yourself acting in some ridiculously negative way, such as totally freaking out and making a fool of yourself in the most stupid ways imaginable. This might seem ludicrous but this is what people do to themselves in their minds. Most people do not even realise that they are doing it to themselves, though. The more you do it, the worse you feel. Of course, this doesn't have to be the way it is. Remember that Chapter 4 says that you get what you focus on, so the more you focus on your panic attacks, the more you will get them. The **first** thing to do instead is to understand that the first panic attack was caused by your body trying to tell you that you needed to relax. You must learn to relax your body and your mind. Using the simple techniques shown in this book will help you. Also, buy some good relaxation music and learn self-hypnosis. The **second** thing to understand is that it isn't the situations that you fear at all but the panic attack. You don't want another one to happen and that is what you fear. The place or situation where it actually occurred is just the thing that was remembered when it first happened. Whenever we get something like a panic attack it is a signal from your body, which is telling you that something is wrong with the way you are living. These signals that we receive — whether it is a headache or palpitation — should not be ignored because if we do, they will become worse. Years ago, I used to suffer from bad headaches. I realise now that that they were signals from my body to tell me that I needed to slow down and relax. When I did, they stopped. And finally the **third** thing to do is to use the Future Behaviour Rehearsal exercise in Chapter 7 twice a day for a least a month to change your associated feelings. And next time your body tries to tell you something, **listen to it**! This treatment strategy can also be used for sexual problems and public speaking.

Smoking

The ultimate self-abuse. Years ago, people weren't told about the dangers of smoking but these days everybody knows about them. People tend to smoke early on, to fit in with friends or to appear more adult. The only problem with that is that once we become a fully-fledged adult we don't have those needs anymore. The only challenge is that we are stuck with the habit. It is **not** a clinical addiction but a psychological addiction. There is a difference. A clinical addiction is what drug addicts have, whereas psychological addiction is merely a habit. Although a powerful habit, it can be removed with the right mindset. The person who truly wants to be a non-smoker must be prepared to make the biggest decision of his or her life. The decision to be a non-smoker cannot be taken lightly; it must be made with full conviction and you must have all the reasons why you want to quit firmly in your mind. Of all the decisions that we make in life, you know that you will never regret the decision to become a non-smoker. You never hear people moan that they feel too healthy or that they have too much money in their pocket after quitting smoking. So you can be sure that the decision to quit is a good one; ask any former smoker. First of all, make a date to quit, then tell yourself you are going to start a challenge involving yourself versus the cigarette company. Tell yourself that the winner of the challenge will dictate your life forever and that **you** will be the winner no matter what happens. What happens after the challenge has begun will be the obstacles within the challenge and you will be ready for them with a show of strength. It's you against the cigarette company and that is your challenge: you either win and become free or you lose and suffer the consequences about which you know only too well. So you must get into the right mindset and begin to get yourself ready for the challenge, knowing that whatever happens after the decision is made and however you feel is the challenge to conquer. To make the transition smoother, I advocate the use of three 1000mg vitamin C tablets a day and two vitamin B complex tablets a day for a month. This is what I extol on my "Quit Smoking" course. Also use the Future Behaviour Rehearsal exercise featured in Chapter 7 twice a day for a least a month to change your associated feelings towards smoking, and do the Changing Bad Habits Exercise in Chapter 1.Cut out the negative chatter (Chapter 2) and **make it work!** Ponder this, do you have a dog? If you do would you give it a cigarette? You probably thinking "Of course not, don't be stupid", so why then would you give yourself one?

Anorexia and bulimia

When a person looks in the mirror and sees a fat person when the scales do not agree, that person is in for a battle. At this point the person involved is thinking with their conscious mind only and is being totally dominated by the nonsense it brings. If they were using their subconscious wisdom it would tell them that they are not fat and that they need to eat properly. When this happens the person who believes the chatter and believes that food is the enemy and that they need to stop eating it or throw it up needs to begin to make some changes urgently. As we have already discussed, for **every behaviour** that we have there is always a payoff. It is not for me to speculate what possible payoffs you might be getting out of this behaviour but what I do know is that whatever the payoff is, it must be stronger than the misery that you are inflicting on yourself and your family. Close your eyes, relax and ask yourself "What is my payoff for this behaviour; what do I get out of it?". Whatever the subconscious mind tells you, understand that it is telling you the truth. You must find an alternative behaviour that gives you the same payoff as the old behaviour used to give you, and do it instead and do it fast! I have heard lots of different reasons when this technique has been used, ranging from "I don't want to grow up" to "I want attention" to "I want to be loved" etc. The need for these payoffs can override the pain of these eating disorders and all the chaos they bring and are at the heart of the problem itself. You need to find an alternative to the old way of receiving the payoff, that has all the same benefits but without the dangerous health consequences. What else can you do instead to receive these same benefits or how might you start to change your perception of the needs that you crave? Every time you say you "can't" do something — whether it's eat food or stop throwing it up — what you are really saying is "I won't". This is because of the **thoughts** you have about what will happen after that and **not** the reality. Remember, "can't" means "won't", so find the payoff and be honest with yourself. Either way, it's time to make a decision. You can either decide to keep on the same track you are on now for the rest of your life and take the consequences that will bring, or decide now to put an end to this madness and do the necessary change techniques outlined next to help you.

Step 1. Decide what you want to do. Do you want to go through the rest of your life living like this?
Step 2. Read through Chapters 2 and 3 again, going through the exercises contained there.
Step 3. Write out your mission statement as described in Chapter 6.
Step 4. Stop reading any material that promotes skinny, unhealthy models. Stop comparing yourself to others and finding fault with yourself, remembering that if you say "I can't" it means that you won't.
After you have decided that you no longer wish to abuse yourself in this way any more, make a commitment never to do so again, no matter what! The conscious mind is the enemy of the eating disorder sufferer.

Depression

There is only one thing that brings about long-term depression and that is **thinking**. The person who is depressed suffers from an overactive conscious mind involvement and thinks about the wrong things. This person focuses on the negative aspects of their past or present and mulls those thoughts over. Sitting at home and "thinking" is definitely a no-go area as this can only lead to more negative analysis. Depressed people see the glass as half-empty and see the negative in everything that happens. They do not appreciate the good things that they do have in life; instead they focus only on the bad. Depression is caused by thinking thoughts that are of no real value and then rethinking them over and over again. This person has allowed the conscious mind to dominate their thinking totally and the garbage it tells them to run riot. The person who suffers depression affects not only themselves but anybody who comes into contact with them, including their long-suffering family. Depression is a **choice**; it is a direction that a person has taken. The affected person doesn't usually know that they have taken it, though, as it seems to have just come over them with time. Depression is a complaint that occurs when a person is **lazy** with their mind. It takes effort to see the good things in life and it is a constant choice to use that mindset. Depression, on the other hand, is caused by not bothering to do that. Not bothering to appreciate life and not being bothered to run your mind correctly. This might outrage the depression sufferer who may deny this and blame a low level of serotonin as the reason but it is nevertheless, in my experience, the truth. Chapter 2 is the key for changing this negative state as the information contained there should be absorbed into your mind as concrete knowledge. Also the Accessing Your Most Resourceful States exercise in Chapter 5 must be practised over and over again until it is **consistent** within yourself. You must stop being lazy with your mind and apply every one of these principles. Now!

Anger and jealousy

These common complaints are once again caused by an overactive conscious mind involvement. The person feeling these emotions is allowing the negative chatter of their conscious mind to run riot. There is no wisdom in this thinking, as crazy conscious mind-driven thoughts are at the forefront of their minds and all common sense has gone out of the window. When people allow themselves to get into this state, the wise subconscious mind tries to help them see sense but the conscious mind often is more dramatic so that they bypass their wisdom and go along with the crazy chatter. The more a person believes and acts upon the negative chatter, the more wound up they become. Often completely over-the-top and inappropriate behaviour is then demonstrated and afterwards the individual is left feeling remorseful and ashamed. Something has to be done about this quickly because prolonged bouts of anger and jealousy usually end up with the person doing it being dumped by their long-suffering partner. Help is at hand in Chapter 2 which deals with how to handle the chatter, which is responsible for the silly thoughts. Go back to this chapter and read it again, doing the exercises. If you think there is cause to be angry or jealous, do not try to figure it out with conscious mind chatter; use the Understanding People Exercise in Chapter 7 and after that use the Future Behaviour Rehearsal exercise in Chapter 7 too. The reason why I suggest this plan of action is because you might have got your wires crossed or maybe you were thinking too selfishly. If a new, different understanding is born, then you must decide to change your behaviour so that future challenges are dealt with wisely. Some people believe that their temper is inherited or even genetic. They are **not**; they are choices. The reason you chose the negative behaviour is because you didn't know any other way to react. You've reacted that way so many times in the past that it just seems right to go the usual way, out of habit. A decision not to go down the old behavioural road is a must in order for any real change to occur, so you must do those two exercises and the Future Behavioural Exercise every day for a week. You must get into the habit of pausing for a few seconds whenever a angry or jealous thought pops into your mind and not reacting straightaway because, if you do, you will probably regret it. Do it now!

Insomnia

In my experience, there are three reasons for insomnia. The first reason is an inability to switch off from the events of the day; the second is a bad habit that became conditioned with repetition; and the third could be chemical. What's on your mind when you try to go to sleep? Are you still thinking about work or are you mulling about the problems in your life? If you are, bedtime is not the time to do it. The time to do it is a couple of hours before you go to bed, so that this bit of business is finished before you sleep. You need to use the Stress Eliminator exercise in Chapter 2 to do this and also the Understanding People exercise in Chapter 7 if applicable. If you are sure that there is nothing going on inside your mind that is affecting your sleep patterns, then it might be simply a bad habit. If you go to bed one night and don't sleep very well, you may then be wary of it happening again the next night. If, on the next night, the same thing happens, you could begin to get anxious and tense as the effects of lack of sleep start to show. The more this cycle happens in this way, the mind and body can begin to lock the thought of sleep into a feeling of tension. The more this cycle is repeated, the more it becomes a self-fulfilling prophecy where the mind starts to condition it into a negative habit.

Instead of thinking about sleep as a nice time to relax and recharge your batteries, the insomniac views it as the start of the battle, so that adrenalin is released into the body to get ready for it. Do not try to beat insomnia, as it will beat you. If you make it a battle, it will win. Instead, try this. As Chapter 4 says, the more you focus on your problems, the worse they will get, so it's time to stop doing that. First of all, have a small glass of milk and a biscuit just before bed. Secondly, when you get into bed don't try to make yourself go to sleep, as this is the habit that we are trying to break. Do not put any pressure on yourself to sleep either as this releases adrenalin which will keep you awake. Thirdly, if you smoke, quit, because the stimulants in nicotine keep you awake. If you won't do that, then at least don't light another one up two hours before bed. Try herbal remedies, as there may be a chemical problem somewhere in the body. I take calcium every night as experts say that one of the symptoms of calcium deficiency is insomnia. Do not look for rapid results with this, though, as vitamins and minerals are not drugs so they are not fast acting. It will probably take at least four months to start to notice any difference. Look forward to sleep as you used to, and break this habit of the big battle. Even if you have to fake this, do it anyway as it is still breaking the habit. Make your time in bed an adventure. I visualise every night in bed just before going to sleep that I am on a journey of some type, whether that is by plane, car, spacecraft or just running. I run this thought, not really knowing where I am going. Every night I start the same process. I decide what means of travel I am going to take and where I want to go, and that isn't limited to Earth either. I run the adventure every night until I am literally bored to sleep. Sometimes it takes ten minutes and other times an hour but I never put conditions on it and I don't care how long it takes. You can make the adventure into anything you like, with any place and any mode of travel and speed. Every now and then everybody has a bad night's sleep It's just one of those things, so don't make a big deal about it and it will happen less.

Low self-esteem

This common complaint is caused by negative self-perception and focus. The person with this challenge will often be able to back up any negative self-criticism with evidence. Instead of looking at their positive points, they bypass them and focus on their "faults". They say things like "I'm dumb" or "I'm ugly", as if by saying those things and continuously thinking those thoughts will actually help them to feel better about themselves! This weak way of using the mind is not only a bore for the person doing it to themselves but it is equally boring to the people who have to listen to them. Do yourself a favour and **get off this track**. Aren't you bored of saying the same boring things to yourself? What good is it doing for you? It's time to think differently and stop pulling yourself down. It's time to stop living your life as if you were in a soap opera and make a decision to stop doing this. People are sick and tired of hearing it and you should be too. This pointless way of thinking is literally wasting your time as every year that passes while in this thinking mode is another one wasted.

Decide now to begin to stop focusing on the things that you don't like about yourself and begin instead to focus and concentrate on your strengths. This may feel a little strange at first but it always does when we change habits. Perseverance is the key. I promise that you will want to keep on doing it. This is not a prescription for being narcissistic; what it is, though, is a healthy new way of thinking and living your life. You've wasted too much of your precious time already making yourself miserable and now it's time to give yourself a break. You must apply the Changing Bad Habits exercise to the thought of staying the same and do it whenever you find yourself criticising yourself. Do it every day whenever you do that for a month and you will have conditioned the change.

Drugs

It doesn't matter what drugs you take, the result is always the same: **negative**. Some drugs will take you to the negative faster than others, though, sometimes so quickly that you die. People take drugs to escape from reality because of an inability to run their brains effectively (see Chapter 2). It's an escape from responsibility where you don't have to think or function in a normal way. The only problem with that is that when you come back to earth your problems have grown bigger. Pretty soon, the drugs are the bigger problem and not the thing that you were using them to escape from. As with smoking, people get into drugs mostly due to peer pressure and they think of their fellow users as family. This "family" is all on the same negative plan where things can only get worse, not better. If you want the type of life where you are succeeding in your goals, you cannot do it with drugs as part of your life. I know of no happy and successful person who uses drugs as a way of life. Think of all the people you know who use drugs. Do you want to be like them?

A lot of drug users will argue that drugs like marijuana are actually quite safe and can always pull out a pretty convincing argument to back up their claims. Look at the people who deny the negative effects of drugs and ask yourself this question: are these people living the kind of life that you would want to live yourself? Do you want to end up like these people? If you do and if you want to amble through life, getting stoned and never amounting to anything, then it's your choice. It's my inclination, though, that if you did, you would not buy a book about personal development and living the best life ever. These people who defend the negative power of drugs waste their lives by never allowing themselves to be any thing else but a pothead. Ask yourself this question: why do I feel the need to escape from reality? If it's your job, marriage or anything else it can be sorted out but it never will be by putting your head in the sand and escaping from reality with drugs. Most people try "soft" drugs as they grow up, as I did, and then move away from them as they mature but there are others who get stuck into the "hard" stuff and lose the plot. For those types the only future is bleak unless they decide to go through withdrawal. If you are one of those people, the principles and exercises in this book can help you but you also need to seek professional help. The question is this: do you want to be a winner or a loser? Do you want to escape from reality or make your own reality, which is real and even more satisfying than pretending with drugs? Food for thought.

Sports performance

If you want to be a good sportsperson, no matter what your sport is, you must practise the Future Behaviour Rehearsal exercise in Chapter 7 in order to really reach your true potential. Most top sportspeople say that the mental side of sport comprises at least 50 per cent of winning. It would be crazy, then, to omit this knowledge and go ahead, leaving your dreams in the lap of the gods. I know of no top-flight sportsperson who does not mentally rehearse the outcomes that they want to achieve. Even if you only want to improve your game, it will certainly improve if you rehearse in the way as described in the Future Behaviour Rehearsal technique in Chapter 7. Also, the negative influence of the conscious mind can easily destroy your self-belief if it is not under your control. You cannot allow the negative influence of the chatter to dictate the results that you achieve.

You must adopt the mindset of **knowing**, rather than hoping, that you will do well. Most people do not like to talk and think so boldly for fear of embarrassment. The thought of things not working out in the way that you had planned is the worry. The mindset of hope is down to bad planning both physically and mentally prior to the sports event in which you wish to participate. I urge you to start talking in the positive rather than using vague language like "I hope" because when you say "I am going to … ", it sends a positive message to your brain. When you say the word "hope" it means that you have doubts about yourself so you must banish any doubts with the exercises in this book if you want to succeed. Self-doubt is nothing more than negative thinking caused by conscious mind chatter and focusing on the wrong things. You must clean up this negative thought process first if you seriously want to be the best that you can be.

The drama queen

Everybody knows one, or maybe you **are** one! The men and women who are drama queens are always in the middle of some crisis where everything is falling apart. Every headache is a tumour and every stomach ache is cancer and sometimes these things become real illnesses brought about by the negative thoughts that they think! When every crisis ends, a new one begins and the performance starts again. Every negative event is magnified by ten and reported with an over-the-top emotional display. Every day is like a new episode of the soap opera where another "curse" is born. Every challenge is a "nightmare" and this person thinks of themselves as life's disaster. The thought "It always happens to me!" is usually followed by an uncontrollable flood of tears and emotions. The person who does this **to themselves** (and yes I did say "**to themselves**") really needs to grow up fast. They tend to think that every drama is the worst point into their lives and will run hysterically to the doctor for instant medication. The need to show everybody how bad things really are with them can verge on an Oscar-winning performance. A five-star performance is always assured as the drama queen proves that there **really is** something wrong with them. Suicide attempts and even psychiatric hospitals are usually next in line as the drama continues. The loved ones who have to suffer this nonsense from these personality types are the ones who really need the break! The story of the boy who cried wolf explains what happens when the dramas go too far and the loved ones stop listening as the same old tune is replayed. The danger, though, is that because the drama queen is no longer listened to, they may seek to gain attention by some stupid means such as a suicide attempt.

This sorry state of affairs can be reversed but the individual doing this to themselves must be brutally honest with themselves. The biggest factors in causing this behaviour are:

1. **The need to gain attention**.
2. **Immaturity.**
3. **Laziness.**

The perpetrator will probably deny this vehemently but nevertheless it is, in my vast experience, the truth. As we discussed earlier, for **every** behaviour, which we exhibit there is a **payoff**. The challenge is, though, that to the drama queen it really **does feel** as if these emotions are things that just happen to them and **not** them doing it to themselves. They will often fiercely argue this point to validate their point and then summon up sudden strength to argue that fact! Funny, isn't it? To some people this may seem a little harsh or insensitive but believe me when I say that everything I do is done for the benefit of the client. If I thought that sympathy was what they needed then this is what I would give them. I am here to help them, not reinforce their immaturity. You could say that they are addicted to the drama. Whenever a client comes to see me with a particular challenge that we sort out and a month or so later they call again, explaining about a new drama popping up, I start to think that something's fishy. If every time I help to solve a problem another one emerges, I know it's time for some tough talking. For drama queens reading this book, know this. It doesn't have to be this way; you **can** break the pattern. Let me show you how:

1. **You must admit that you have been an impossible pain in the ass and that it's time to make a change in yourself. Apologise to all concerned and tell them that you are now a changed person who takes full responsibility for yourself.**
2. **It's time to make some decisions, so run through the Changing Bad Habits exercise in Chapter 1. Make the**

decision to be proactive for the rest of your life and stop living this charade.

3. **Apply each and every philosophy and exercise in this book and install them into your personality. Not for a week or a month but forever, and set about a new mission constantly to develop yourself in every positive way possible.**
4. **Become a doer and not a complainer. Read through the five characteristics of dynamic people in this book and do whatever it takes to live your life in the same way. Become an inspiration to the people you meet and become completely the opposite of what you are now.**

Obviously, to make these kinds of changes is going to take a little time. And doing these things will feel that you are going totally against the grain of things but **have the conviction** that you will see it through no matter what or how strange it feels. You have the rest of your life to get this right, so it's O.K. to make mistakes along the way as long as you learn from them. Now, take a deep breath, shake your body and get on with it — you've got work to do.

I have outlined the most common problems that people have today. If you have a challenge that is not listed above, do not worry, as the same strategies apply to all. The symptoms outlined in this chapter and others are pretty irrelevant and it doesn't matter what they are, whether they are lack of self- confidence or a fear of spiders. **Every challenge that we encounter is caused by an inability to run our own minds correctly.** Whenever you don't run your mind correctly, it will result in some kind of symptom. The symptom is to tell you that you're not running your mind correctly. You must begin to learn how to run your mind rather than letting it run you. What symptom is invented because of that is not important; it could have been anything.

How the symptoms affect you is what you don't like and it all boils down to the same thing. This whole book gives clues for solving every challenge that you could possibly face. You may have grasped what the source of all of these challenges is but, if you haven't yet, let me spell it out for you:

YOUR MIND IS THE KEY TO EVERYTHING!

Thank you for reading this book. I hope that one day we will meet but, until we do:

LIVE THE BEST LIFE EVER!

Acknowledgements

There are many people who have helped me to get to the point in life where I am now. I would like to acknowledge those people now and thank them for the valuable information they have shared with me. If you are one of those people, NO DOUBT you will have spotted your own influence throughout this book. You can feel proud that your work is being passed on and has indeed inspired others to help others just like you did. To name you all would probably fill another book so I have decided to mention those who have been the greatest influence on me:

Anthony Robbins; Richard Carlson; Dr Wayne Dyer; Richard Bandler; Deepak Chopra; Dr Joel Wallach; Ed Foreman; Paul McKenna; Dennis Rush; Frank Thompson and too many more to mention.

Suggested reading

Anything from Dr Wayne Dyer, Richard Carlson, Anthony Robbins, Ed Foreman, and anybody else who gives positive, constructive wisdom on how to live life to the full.

Remember that continuous personal development is the key to your continuing success.

Visit www.freeyourmind.info
Or
www.nortonhypnotherapy.com
to contact me personally.

Index of Exercises

<u>The Principles of Life At a glance</u>

1.You Own You: Every person I have ever met who are truly happy, and successful, are all Proactive. What it means is that **<u>they know</u>** that **<u>they are responsible</u>** for their own happiness, their lives and their futures. They **never blame** circumstances, or events in the past for their own or problems instead they understand that we they can only affect us if we choose to be affected by them. See mistakes as learning experiences, or opportunities to learn. Say "***What can I learn from this***" when things don't work out how you want them to. Mistakes are the stepping- stones to your ***<u>eventual</u>*** success! The past **<u>does not</u>** equal the future so leave the past in the past and move on. You don't have to repeat the past. You are not a robot.

2.Your Thoughts Control Your Feelings: That's right, you are, nobody else. Remember you can't feel upset if you don't first think upsetting thoughts, **don't** take your negative thoughts so seriously, think of them as "Chatter" and learn to dismiss them. You do have the choice, you can let them affect you or not. Thinking that our parents, partners, being rich or the world changing will make us happy is a prescription for unhappiness and disappointment! It's our **<u>thoughts</u>** not circumstances that control our feelings. Your thoughts control the way you feel, so <u>be careful what you think about.</u> Understand that **<u>we</u>** make <u>ourselves</u> happy by the thoughts we think. Don't expect others to think like you do. Remember **moods** are chemical based, caused by chemical fluctuations in the body and NOT the circumstances of your life. **<u>Don't analyse</u>** your life when you are in such a chemically induced mood and it will pass sooner.

3. Your Beliefs Make Your World: There is no greater influence in our lives than our beliefs. We see what we believe. We need to get rid of **ALL** of our negative beliefs as if we don't we will drag them around with us forever affecting the outcomes we get. We become what we believe we are. What we can or can't do is so because of our beliefs. Begin to **doubt old negative beliefs** like *"I can't be happy" or "I can't change"* and so on, and then chuck them in your mental bin as we make them up anyway. We cannot afford to hold onto **ANY** negative beliefs about ourselves we must put in place some new powerful and positive ones.

4. You Get More of What You Focus on: The more you focus on your problems, the more BIGGER they become. It's time for a **NEW FOCUS** in your life. Something dramatically different, something exiting or challenging (and fun). Today!! Make health your priority, **look after your self,** exercise, eat well, **stay young** and develop a thirst for knowledge. Don't buy into that "as you get older things get harder to learn" rubbish! Your brain is like a muscle it needs to be exercised with new varied bits of information not what's happening in your favourite soap opera. When the brain isn't used enough it gets bored and will create problems to give you a bit of "Drama". **Don't** live your life like it's a drama, getting over upset and dramatic over the smallest things, **take a deep breath relax and learn to centre your thoughts.**

5.Remember Happiness is a STATE: Find your code. Use the posture or physiology of confidence. Stand or sit that way, breathe that way, talk that way, look that way, do it **consistently.** When you do this your body sends a message to your nervous system which tells your brain "**I'M CONFIDENT**"! When ever your not feeling very confident notice your posture and voice tone I bet it's not good. Change it into your position of Confidence. Tone up your voice! Don't feel the need to tell every body about every negative thing that happened in your day, **you don't have to relive it** again, and infect them and either!

6. Create the Life you Want: Write it down, about what your goal/s are for your life. What moves you? What inspires you? What is your true purpose in this world anyway? How do you want to be remembered when your gone? Find your **passion**!! Look forward to new challenges and be curious about them, get exited about them and enjoy learning about yourself "How good can I be, how far can I take myself "? Delete the words **"CAN'T"** or **"but what if"** from your vocabulary.

7. Stop Letting Your Mind Poison You! : Don't just listen to that negative chatter belittle you tell it to SHUT UP! You're the boss, tell it loud and clear it's opinion is bulls#@t. Tell your self **you are super- confidant.** Visualise positive outcomes on a daily basis; let your mind see what you **want to happen**, rather than dreaming up totally ridiculous negative consequences that will never happen! Your mind is goal-orientated machines so don't plan to fail. When you look for what's wrong in your life you will find it. Don't let miserable people influence you; what they say is their opinion **NOT** fact!!

8. Enjoy Yourself: Lighten up, loosen up, and cut your self some slack (stop being so bloody serious and **ENJOY YOUSELF!**) Remember your not perfect nobody is, see problems as challenges to conquer. Stop "**mind reading**" you don't know what they're thinking about you. We find life is dull and boring primarily to dull boring people! Learn to value yourself, b**e at peace** with your little faults. Remember there is no way to Happiness, Happiness **IS** a choice. Simplify your life.